Maurice Sendak

LITERATURE FROM CRESCENT MOON PUBLISHING

Rethinking Powys: Critical Essays on John Cowper Powys
edited by Jeremy Mark Robinson

The Ecstasies of John Cowper Powys
by A.P. Seabright

Postmodern Powys: New Essays on John Cowper Powys
by Joe Boulter

Thomas Hardy and John Cowper Powys: Wessex Revisited
by Jeremy Mark Robinson

Sexing Hardy: Thomas Hardy and Feminism
by Margaret Elvy

Thomas Hardy's Jude the Obscure: A Critical Study
by Margaret Elvy

Thomas Hardy's Tess of the d'Urbervilles: A Critical Study
by Margaret Elvy

Thomas Hardy: The Tragic Novels
by Tom Spenser

Stepping Forward: Essays, Lectures and Interviews
by Wolfgang Iser

Lawrence Durrell: Between Love and Death
by Jeremy Mark Robinson

Andrea Dworkin
by Jeremy Mark Robinson

German Romantic Poetry: Goethe, Novalis, Heine, Hölderlin
by Carol Appleby

Cavafy: Anatomy of a Soul
by Matt Crispin

Rilke: Space, Essence and Angels in the Poetry
by B.D. Barnacle

Rimbaud: Arthur Rimbaud and the Magic of Poetry
by Jeremy Mark Robinson

Shakespeare: Love, Poetry and Magic in Shakespeare's Sonnets and Plays
by B.D. Barnacle

Feminism and Shakespeare
by B.D. Barnacle

The Poetry of Landscape in Thomas Hardy
by Jeremy Mark Robinson

D.H. Lawrence: Infinite Sensual Violence
by M.K. Pace

D.H. Lawrence: Symbolic Landscapes
by Jane Foster

The Passion of D.H. Lawrence
by Jeremy Mark Robinson

Samuel Beckett Goes Into the Silence
by Jeremy Mark Robinson

In the Dim Void: Samuel Beckett's Late Trilogy: Company, Ill Seen, Ill Said and Worstward Ho
by Gregory Johns

Andre Gide: Fiction and Fervour in the Novels
by Jeremy Mark Robinson

Julia Kristeva: Art, Love, Melancholy, Philosophy, Semiotics
by Kelly Ives

Luce Irigaray: Lips, Kissing, and the Politics of Sexual Difference
by Kelly Ives

Hélène Cixous I Love You: The Jouissance of Writing
by Kelly Ives

Petrarch, Dante and the Troubadours
by Cassidy Hughes

Friedrich Hölderlin: *Selected Poems*
translated by Michael Hamburger

Rainer Maria Rilke: *Selected Poems*
translated by Michael Hamburger

Maurice Sendak Pocket Guide

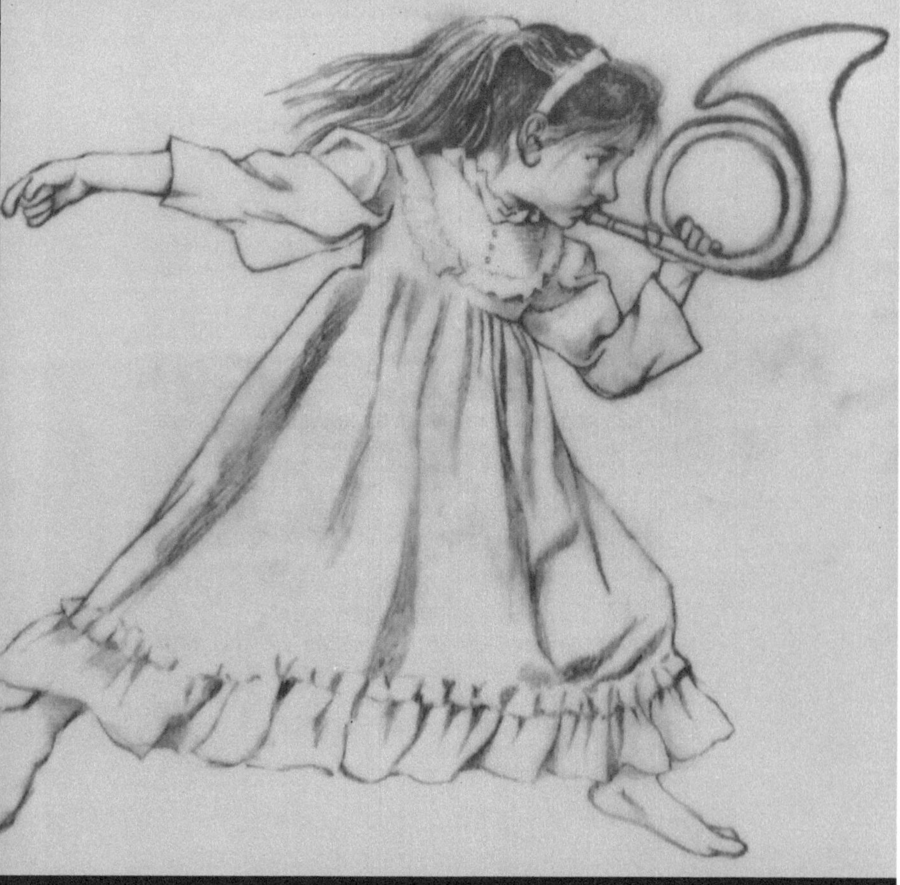

L.M. Poole

CRESCENT MOON

CRESCENT MOON PUBLISHING
P.O. Box 1312, Maidstone
Kent, ME14 5XU
Great Britain
www.crmoon.com

First published 2013.

Printed and bound in the U.S.A.
Set in Helvetica Neue Condensed 9 on 12pt.
Designed by Radiance Graphics.

British Library Cataloguing in Publication data

Poole, L.M.
Maurice Sendak: Pocket Guide
1. Sendak, Maurice, 1928-2012 –Criticism and interpretation
2. Children's literature – Illustrations
3. Illustration of books – United States – 20th century
I. Title II. Sendak, Maurice, 1928-2012

741.6'42'092

ISBN-13 9781861713087

Contents

Acknowledgements

Thanks to Maurice Sendak.

Illustrations © Maurice Sendak. Thanks to copyright holders of other illustrations, including HarperCollins, Publishers, Inc, Warner Bros., Penguin, Harper & Row, Holt, Rinehart & Winston, Farrar, Straus & Giroux, Collier, Viking Kestrel, Crown, Macmillan, Linnet, Candlewick, Oxford University Press, M. K. McElderry, and The Bodley Head.

Abbreviations

C	*Caldecott & Co.*
W	*Where the Wild Things Are*
I	*In the Night Kitchen*
O	*Outside Over There*
DM	*Dear Mili*
MJ	*The Moon Jumpers*
JT	*The Juniper Tree*
NL	*The Nutshell Library*
S	*The Sign On Rosie's Door*
F	*Fly By Night*
SLM	*Seven Little Monsters*
SSP	*Some Swell Pup*
H	*Higglety Pigglety Pop!*
HP	*Hector Protector*
AMS	*The Art of Maurice Sendak* (by Selma G. Lanes)
AMS2	*The Art of Maurice Sendak* (by Tony Kushner)

To enliven all is the aim of life

Novalis

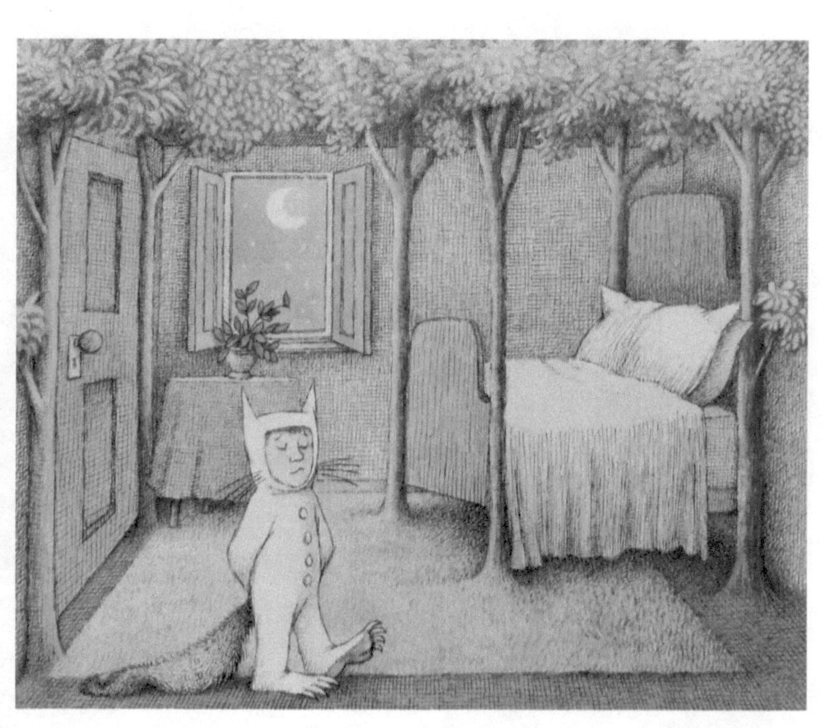

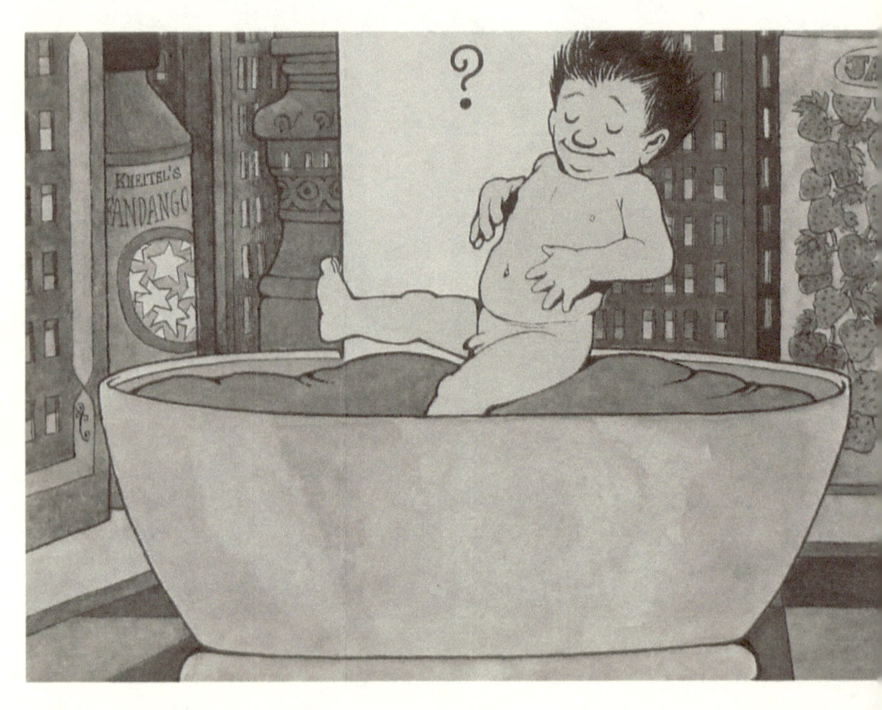
KNEITEL'S
FANDANGO

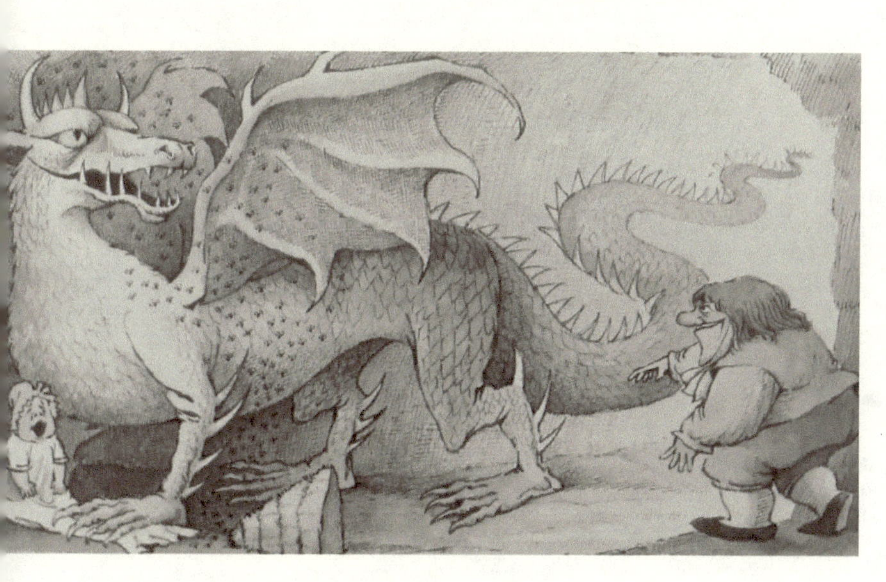

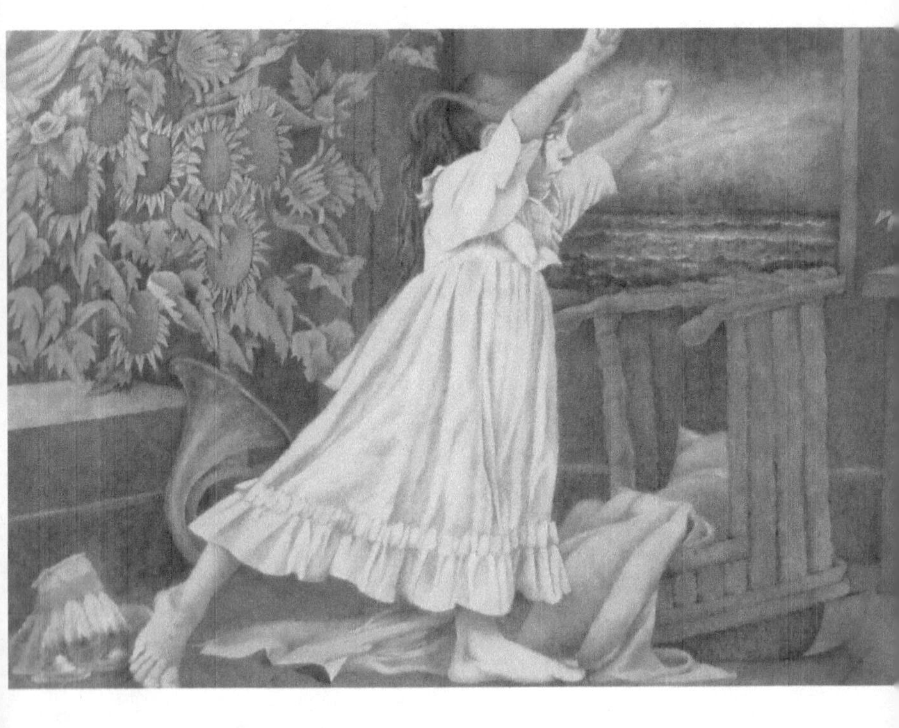

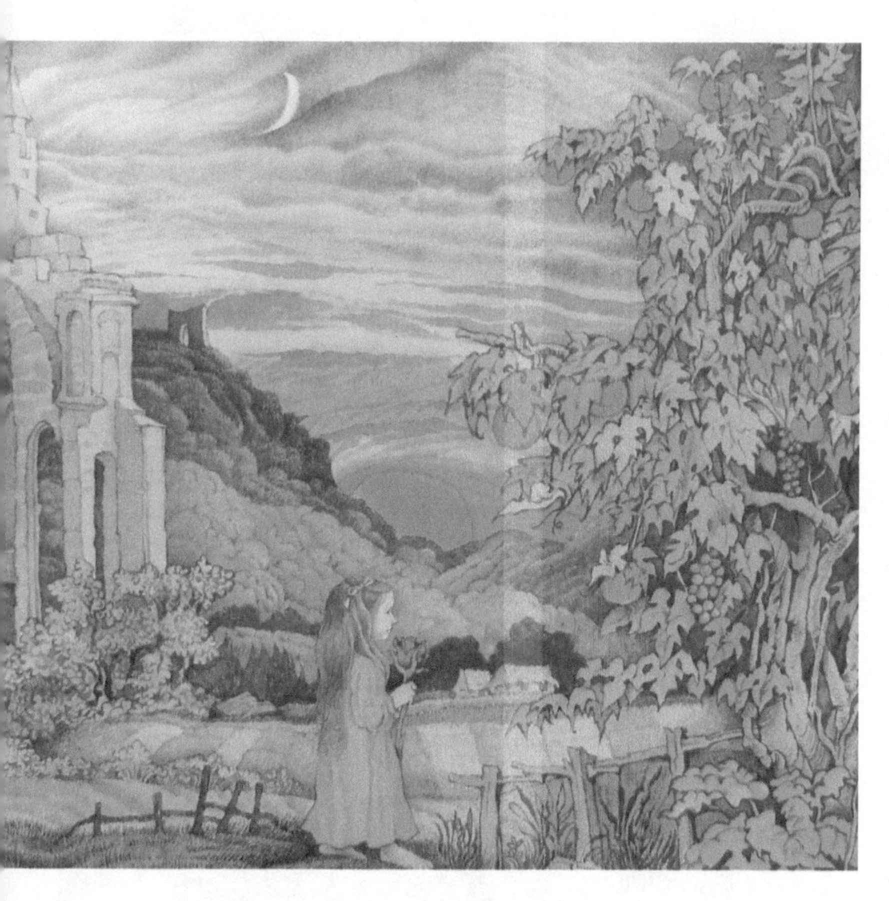

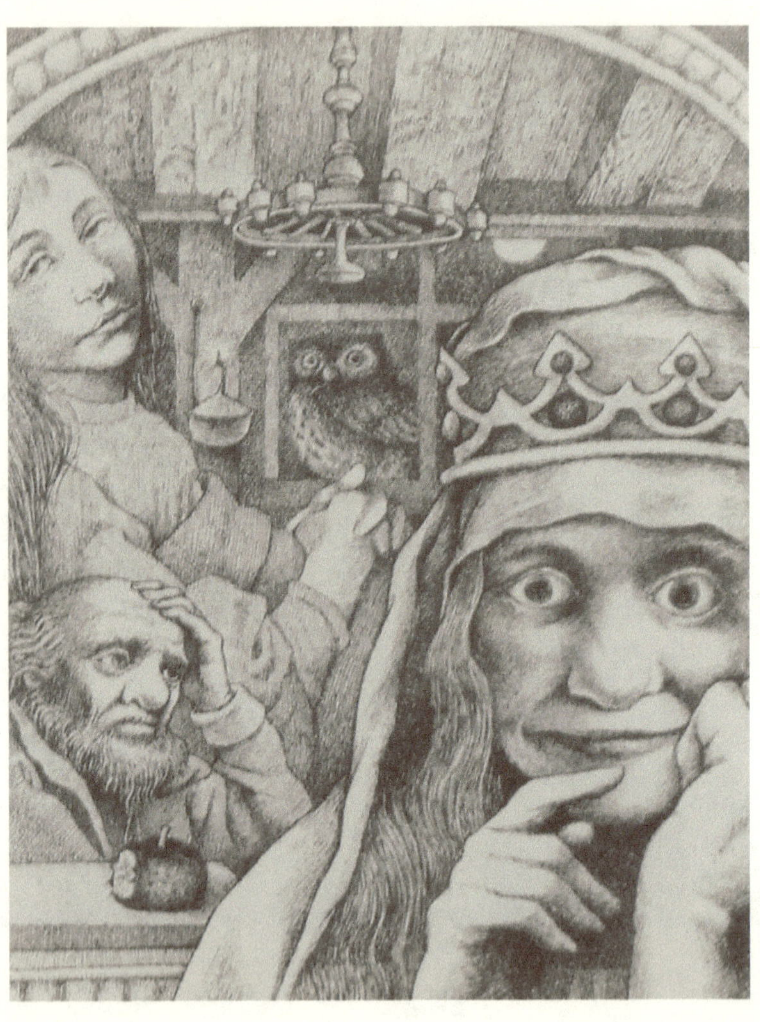

I

Introduction

I am trying to draw the way children feel – or, rather, the way I imagine they feel. It's the way I know *I felt as a child. And all I have to go on is what I know – not only about my childhood then, but about the child I was as he exists now. My most unusual gift is that my child-self seems still to be alive and well.*

Maurice Sendak (AMS, 27, 265)

MAURICE SENDAK (1928-2012), has become America's premier children's book author and illustrator. He's as important – and as adored – as Theodore Geisel (Dr Seuss). Best known for his trilogy of classic children's picture books – *Where the Wild Things Are* (1963), *In the Night Kitchen* (1970) and *Outside Over There* (1981) – Maurice Sendak has also written many other books (though mainly in the children's book form). His interpretation of the Grimm Brothers, 1973's *The Juniper Tree*, although it is less well-known, could be said to be his most accomplished work.

My book aims to consider some of Maurice Sendak's significant works, concentrating on the children's books and the picture books. Other chapters explore Sendak's relationship with the movies and art of Walt Disney (which Sendak admires); his interpretation of classic fairy tales; a brief consideration of the fairy tale form; Sendak's links with the tradition of children's book illustration; and finally a comparison of Sendak's art with that of other book illustrators.

The Oxford Companion to Children's Literature offers a typical assessment of Maurice Sendak as one of the highpoints of modern children's book illustration:

> *Quite apart from his outstanding draughtsmanship and mastery of styles, Sendak's exploration of the realms of the unconscious in* Where the Wild Things Are *and its successors lifts his work beyond the confines of the children's picture book and places it among major art of the 20th century.*[6]

Joyce Whalley and Tessa Chester write of Maurice Sendak in *A History of Children's Book Illumination*:

> *Sendak's superiority amounts to far more than mere technical ability and an instinct for interpreting a text, whether his own or that of someone else. His sympathy and concern with every book he illustrates mounts to an almost religious obsession when it comes to his own picture books... His vision is unique, his draughtsmanship par excellence, and his work as a whole lifts him well into the ranks of the great illustrators of all time.* (236)

Lee Kingman is equally laudatory, calling Maurice Sendak 'a magician who, working on several levels simultaneously, creates a world of carefully wrought surfaces and spaces dense with suggested drama.' (1978, 79)

A friend of mine, Alison Dunworth, called her only child Max, after the hero of *Where the Wild Things Are.* She loved the book. The impression the book made on her as a child was so great that, when it came to naming her first (and only) child, it had to be Max. (It's a familiar story: so many fans and readers have encountered Sendak's art at a young and impressionable age, and they never forget it).

The names of Maurice Sendak's protagonists are similarly crucial. Sendak clearly muses upon his names deeply: Max, Mickey, Ida – they are simple names, but, for Sendak, as for any poet, names must resonate in *precisely* the right way ('Sendak' means 'fish', Sendak said). Not just *any* name will do. The name must have the right connotations. Sendak's characters' names are not the posh (English) names of the bourgeoisie: Martine, Charlotte, Christine, Justine, Joachim, André or Patrick. Rather, they are simple, homely names, such as Kate, Kelly, Rose, Lou, Minnie and Cassie, and Sam, Tom, Charlie and Jamie. They might come out of Mark Twain. They are the simple names of fairy tales: Hans, Jack, Ivan, Tom, Else, Gretel.

One name, in particular, is important to Maurice Sendak: *Mickey*, because of Mickey Mouse. In *TV Guide* (1978) Sendak reveals, again, his close identification with Mickey Mouse: '[t]his year, Mickey Mouse and I will be celebrating our fiftieth birthday.'[1] Sendak goes on to note how he and Mickey Mouse share the same initial letter, 'M'. Mickey is clearly a special name for Sendak, so special that in the 'personal' (i.e. autobiographical) book *In the Night Kitchen*, he called the hero Mickey (and another 'M' name, Max, is the hero of *Where the Wild Things Are*).

Names in fairy tales are significant: fairies disappear when the name of Jesus or God is uttered; fairies are sometimes referred to by an alternative, as their actual name can be unlucky (in Ireland they're called *sidhe*, the Good Folk, in Celtic lore they are the Hill Folk, in England and Germany they are the Kleine Volk or Little Folk); in many religions the name of a god or God is taboo; in Christianity names have a superstitious power – a child's name is not announced before baptism, as a protection against bad spirits or witches; new or second names are given to children and young adults at initiation rituals; the second or 'spiritual' birth (or rebirth) often requires a new name; some names can work magic, such as the *Open Sesame* of Ali Baba, or the ancient Hebrew *abracadabra*; in *Rumpelstiltskin* it is the name itself that destroys the dwarf (in English folk tales there is *Tom Tit Tot*, from East Anglia, while in Cornwall the Devil appears as Terry-top; in Scotland the name is Whuppity Stoorie; in Austria Kruzimugeli, in Spain Marie Kirikitou, and in Iceland Gilitrutt).

The snobbishness that surrounds characters' names also extends to the hegemony of physical attributes. American children's book illustrations for a long time only portrayed squeaky-clean All-American types. That is, blonde, blue-eyed and white, perfectly proportioned youths. In the 1950s some people thought Maurice Sendak's children, with their fat little bodies and dark hair, repulsive. By the early 1970s, though, such was the success of Sendak's type of character that, Ursula Nordstrom noted, all real children looked like Sendak's illustrations of children.[2]

It's the same with the story title, and each of Maurice Sendak's titles, like *Alice's Adventures in Wonderland,* are instant classics. *Where the Wild Things Are* is immediately a great title. Firstly, it sounds like a children's book title. Secondly, it targets the whole trajectory of the story, which is a journey or quest to where the wild things live. And it puts the journey into the present. Not *Where the Wild Things Were*, but *Where the Wild Things Are*. It's a title that recalls the magic phrase that mediæval mapmakers used to put on the very edge of their maps: *Here Be Dragons.* Indeed, there *are* dragons, right now, just as there *are* wild things. And it is *to* the place of the wild things, to where the wild things are, that we go in Sendak's magical story.

But it is also to the place where the wild things are that one goes in so much of children's fiction, and in so much of art. For 'where the wild things are' is the nighttime place, the place of dreams, of fears, of anxieties.[3] It is dreamland, a place both dazzling and dark, a place of wildness. It is the place not only of fantasy, not only of fantasy art and literature, but of much of art and literature.[4] It's also called the 'secondary world' or 'fantasy world'. It is the place the witches conjure up in *Macbeth*; it is the place of much of Hollywood's movie output; it is the place of so much literature. Feminists have spoken of a female 'wild zone', a place outside of men's experience and patriarchal art, a place special to women's experience and feminine culture.[5] In a similar way, Maurice

Sendak creates a 'wild zone', which is not the 'wild zone' of men or women.

It might be trite and stupid to cite moments in Maurice Sendak's childhood and relate them to illustrations in his books. I've never liked that sort of biographical analysis, which says, 'Oh, X tripped on a rabbit hole when he was five and nearly broke his leg. And that's why rabbit holes feature so prominently in X's work.' (Such as: J.R.R. Tolkien was bitten by a spider in South Africa as a child, which's why nasty spiders appear in his fiction). That sort of biography is too easy.

There are moments in Maurice Sendak's biography, however, which reveal him to be a yearning, wistful sort of boy, who loved going to New York City from Brooklyn, who found enchantment in the darkened cinemas in the 1930s, who idolized his older sister, and who believed in angels. To cite one biographical moment, to show that sense of magic so important in Sendak's work, described by Selma Lanes:

> *Angels were active participants in most of Philip's* [Sendak's father's] *stories, and Sendak attributes his fondness for them from his father. Indeed, he remembers his father's telling him once when he was sick that if stared hard enough out the window he might see an angel flying by. If he did, it was a sign of good luck and he would get better quickly. "But, if you blink, you'll miss it," his father told him. After Philip left the room, the boy stared as hard as he could for minutes at a time. Suddenly, he thought he saw an angel. He screamed for his father, "I saw it, I saw it!" And Sendak remembers his father's pleasure when he rushed back into the room. "He was as thrilled as I was."* (*The Art of Maurice Sendak*, hereafter as AMS, 12-13)

Easy to see why people point to Maurice Sendak's childhood for the roots of his art. For instance, beds feature a lot in his work, and he spent much of his time sick in bed during his childhood. Or to look at his *shtetl* Brooklyn environment and 'the Old World reverberations' (AMS, 26), and find it in his Brothers Grimm illustrations. (In a way, all the mothers in

Sendak's art are drawn from his own mother, and all the young girls are inspired by his sister Natalie. And his babies are based on himself). Sendak of course draws on his own childhood for his art:

> *I am trying to draw the way children feel – or, rather, the way I imagine they feel. It's the way I* know *I felt as a child. And all I have to go on is what I know – not only about my childhood then, but about the child I was as he exists now. My most unusual gift is that my child-self seems still to be alive and well.* (AMS, 27, 265)

What Maurice Sendak has done in his art is to capture some of the feelings of childhood more piquantly than most other illustrators. It is partly this which makes him successful. To put it simply, Sendak is an artist who keeps in touch with the feelings of childhood. For instance, when Fall comes around, Sendak, just like a child, thinks about when the first snow will fall so he can go sledging. In way, Sendak doesn't believe the child he was ever grew up, or became the person he is.

> *He still exists somewhere, in the most graphic, plastic, physical way for me* [Sendak said]. *I have a tremendous concern for, and interest in, him. I try to communicate with him all the time. One of my worst fears is losing contact. The pleasures I get as an adult are heightened by the fact that I experience them as a child at the same time.* (AMS, 27)

✪

Among Maurice Sendak's artistic friends were Philip Roth, Twla Tharp, Marianne Moore, Grace Paley, Randall Jarrell, Coleman Dowell, Jules Feiffer and Tony Kushner. His partner for 50 years was Dr Eugene Glynn (d. 2007).

For Tony Kushner, Sendak could be 'complex, contradictory, mercurial, wickedly funny, exasperating, erudite, generous, entirely unique, and the source of so much glorious art' (AMS2, 193).

The elements of Jewish culture in Maurice Sendak's art

(and biography) have been somewhat neglected in Sendak criticism. Tony Kushner calls Sendak a product of the Great Depression and of Jewish Depression, that conviction,

> *passed through hundreds of generations, that true home is elsewhere, promised but not attained, perhaps not even attainable. Maurice's is a Yiddische kopf, a large, brooding, circumspect, and contemplative mind, darkened by both fatalism and faith.* (AMS2, 190)

The way that Sendak composes his texts and poetry, the way it employs a rhythm and meter, is particularly Jewish for Tony Kushner, who stresses Sendak's Jewishness in his book (AMS2, 204).

II

Children's Book Illustration

MAURICE SENDAK'S FAVOURITE illustrators are Randolph Caldecott (1846-86), Boutet de Monvel (1855-1913), Wilhelm Busch (1832-1908), Hans Fischer and André François (1915-2005) (quoted in *Caldecott & Co.,* hereafter as C, 146). Sendak also speaks warmly of British artists William Blake ('unquestionably important, my cornerstone in many ways' [AMS, 185]), George Cruikshank (1792-1878), one of the great 19th century British book illustrators, Samuel Palmer (1805-81), the British landscape painter, Otto Ubbelohde (1867-1922) and Thomas Rowlandson (1756-1827, creator of extraordinary erotica) (C, 171). Among writers, he has cited Emily Dickinson, D.H. Lawrence, Herman Melville, John Keats, Blake and William Shakespeare (AMS2, 65). Jean-Jacques Rousseau was another thinker that Sendak admired.

The weight and legacy of 19th century and early 20th century children's illustration can be discerned behind all of Maurice Sendak's output Sendak happily borrowed from other artists' work: he used direct quotes from the art of Albrecht Dürer, Philipp Otto Runge and Auguste Rodin, for instance.[1] Sendak also took up – most clearly in *The Juniper Tree* – the early woodcutters' practice of choosing the decisive moments in a story. Most book illustrators have done the same, commented D. Bland in *A History of Book Illustration* (1958, 164).

19th century book illustration for children's books, such as collections of fairy tales, was very much a male or masculinist preserve. The beginnings of fairy tale illustration occurred largely in Western Europe (France, Germany, Britain), and North America. The great names of 19th century illustrators – Gustave Doré, Thomas Bewick, Ludwig Grimm, George Cruikshank, Ludwig Richter – are all male. The fairy tale industry was a masculine business. Men (and masculine culture) were the mediators and interpreters of fairy tales. The reading audience was largely bourgeois and aristocratic.

Children's book illustrators were subject to the same levels of censorship, conventions and morality as novelists or painters. There were certain things that could not be said or shown, just as today. Charles Perrault's tales and then the Grimms' oral, folk and fairy tales were gradually censored and cleaned up. (This sweetening reached its highpoint with Walt Disney's feature films.) The 19th century is often celebrated as the highpoint of (children's) book illustration: it was also the age of widespread suppression – pregnancy and abortion could not be mentioned in popular magazines; under the surface, there was mass prostitution and pornography. (The 21st century is thought of as 'permissive', 'liberated', and so on, but there are still plenty of images that cannot be shown.)

Maurice Sendak's own books have been criticized in terms of morality and 'decency' – his gloriously naked Mickey in *In the Night Kitchen* was thought unsuitable for young children by some. It sure is odd, anti-censorship advocates claim, when nakedness and the body itself is censored (how can you censor the foundation of all human life, the body?). For the pro-censorship lobby, linking children with nudity in popular culture is increasingly problematic. (For some critics, Sendak hasn't been able at times to resist upsetting the authorities who jealousy guard children's book literature.)

Children's book illustration sits in an ambiguous space somewhere between fine art and commercial hackwork. Clearly, illustrators such as Maurice Sendak, Kate Greenaway, Arthur Rackham, John Tenniel, Gustave Doré, etc, would probably prefer to be valued as fine art, real art, not a mere commercial product. Yet few children's book illustrations work on their own, away from of the book, put on a wall and framed. Virtually anything by Gustave Doré, Aubrey Beardsley or Arthur Rackham can be thus detached from the story and shown on their own. Many of Sendak's pictures, too, can be isolated and still have their own life (the wild rumpus pictures, from *Where the Wild Things Are,* for example, were used for Penguin's publicity material, and did just fine – they have become iconic in popular culture). Most children's book illustrations, though, need the rhythms, pacing, story and context of a particular book to make them flourish. In discussing one particular picture, one must always be aware of the others before and after it, and of the whole story.

Maurice Sendak further emphasizes the unity of a book by having clues early on in the book to what happens later (the Wild-Thing-like doll in the first picture, and the picture of the monster on the wall 'by Max', which presages the Wild Things, for example). The final pictures in a Sendak book often mirror the first pictures (in *Outside Over There* and *Dear Mili* for example).

WORDS FIRST

MAURICE SENDAK BEGINS not with the pictures, as one might expect, but with the words. He has explained on a number of occasions that his written texts have to be 'very good before he considers illustrating them.' (1979, 31) The words are essential, they locate the pictures within a particular narrative, context and meaning. The words 'anchor' the pictures into a dominant or preferred set of meanings, which Sendak likes to get right first (C, 176). 'I like to think of myself as setting words to pictures. A true picture book is a visual poem', he remarked (AMS, 110). (It's interesting that Jacob Grimm was not only the writer of one of the most influential books in fairy tale literature, *Children's and Household Tales*, he was also 'perhaps the greatest of all philologists', as Tom Shippey pointed out.[2] Language and philology were thus fundamental to fairy tale culture).

Maurice Sendak's concern with words also reminds us of his emphasis on storytelling. All Sendak's books are narrative books, books which move from one point in a story to another. The pictures, though, must not merely illustrate the words. The pictures must always do more than that. The words must allow for an openness of interpretation in the pictures. The two, words and pictures, work in tandem, but not merely mirror each other (C, 185). The written text, if it's a good one, will leave gaps of meaning into which the pictures can be inserted. There must be an ambiguity to what is happening in the written text too, so that the text can function on a number of levels. It is the conscious working at this split-level meaning that marks Sendak out from other illustrators. His books always have a carefully cultivated symbolic dimension: they are never merely descriptions of physical deeds (*Miss X walked upstairs, sat down and opened her diary*, etc).

As an example of narrative openness, Maurice Sendak cites the *Mother Goose* nursery rhymes, which often have a political or religious subtext (for instance, 'Oranges and Lemons', or, famously, 'Ring-a-Ring-a-Roses', which is about the Plague in mediæval Europe). At the same time, the pictures, in Sendak's view, must be able to exist on their own, they must be somewhat independent of the written story. A good picture book can be consumed just by looking at the pictures. Many young children, below reading age, do this: leaf through books without considering the written text. For Sendak, as a maker, an artist, the words are important, but for the young child, the pictures take precedence. Books such as *Where the Wild Things Are* and *In the Night Kitchen* are *picture* books, not written texts. The pictures are printed as large as possible on the page, and the words seem to be secondary, from the point-of-view of a young, pre-school age reader.

✪

In all his writings, Maurice Sendak stresses the art of illustration as nothing less than a 'mystic rite'. Illustrating for him means:

> *having a passionate affair with the words. I hate to say it's akin to a mystic rite, but there is no other language to describe what happens. It is a sensual, deeply important experience.* (AMS, 109)

Maurice Sendak uses space as economically as he can: every inch of space has something in it. The problems of squeezing so much of a story into one frame means the result can be crowded, as in the illustration in *Fitcher's Feathered Bird* from Sendak's interpretation of the Grimms, *The Juniper Tree*, where around the two figures we see a skull, a key, two trees, and the house with the skull in the window. If the *Fitcher's Feathered Bird* picture seems overcrowded, the illustration for *Rabbit's Bride* in *The Juniper Tree* is packed with figures. Here Sendak's sense of the macabre or Gothic expresses itself. The head of the rabbit assumes a ghastly prominence in the illustration, looking as if it would be more at home in *Alice's Adventures in Wonderland.* While the rabbit's head dominates the picture, if you look closer you see that the rabbit is embracing a scarecrow, whose head is constructed from a mass of straw tied together. This is not all: for behind the rabbit is a fox – in the finished picture it wears glasses (it is without glasses in the sketch for the story). Next to the fox, a large bird, possibly a crow. Sendak's 'darker' pictures suggest comparisons with the 'darker' creators of art: painters such as Leonardo da Vinci, Gustave Moreau or Hieronymous Bosch, whose *The Garden of Earthly Delights* remains unsurpassed as a vision of the grotesque (Salvador Dali, Arnold Böcklin, Henry Fuseli and Félicien Rops have not improved on Bosch's bizarre visions, despite trying very hard).

Painful though Maurice Sendak might have found it to do his Grimm pictures, he produced his best work. The very limitations of the single illustration for each story set him free. The sense of the macabre or uncanny (*unheimlich*) is never far away in Sendak's art. In the shadowy corners monsters can be lurking. But figures do not have to be monsters to be frightening in Sendak's art. He turns seemingly 'ordinary' humans into unsettling figures. The most obviously dramatic example of an image from the horror genre is the Devil in *Grandmother's Tale* in *Zlateh the Goat and Other Stories,* which looks forward to Sendak's Brothers Grimm pictures. Sendak's East European Devil would scare many young children. He sticks his tongue out and leers obscenely at the viewer. But even when Sendak is appearing to be fluffy and cuddly, as in the pictures to *A Kiss For Little Bear*, by Else Minarik (1968), Sendak is not completely light-hearted. The picture of the grandmother bear is not the typical lightweight fodder of children's books (Sendak said he used to examine his grandmother 'all the time and place her in various fantasies' as a child [AMS, 16]).

MAURICE SENDAK'S WORKS AS 'CLASSICS'

MAURICE SENDAK'S BOOKS have become 'classic', but thousands and thousands of children's books do not make it anywhere near 'classic' or re-read. Picture books have to survive in a competitive environment of endless televisual imagery; toystores full of images; comics; stickers; posters; magazines; films; merchandizing; food packaging; i-Pods; cell phones; the internet; computer games, and so on. Out of this overwhelming surge of imagery, somehow, John Tenniel's *Alice's Adventures in Wonderland* images survive, and Babar, Mickey Mouse, Beatrix Potter's Peter Rabbit, Heinrich Hoffmann's 'Little Suck-a-Thumb', Edward Lear's *Book of Nonsense*, Enid Blyton's Noddy, and Postman Pat. To these enduring classics of children's literature, we must also add Sendak's Max,

Mickey and Rosie.

What is it about a particular book that makes it a children's classic? As Nina Mikkelsen writes in "Sendak, Snow-White and the Child as Literary Critic", what 'causes four year old Lolly to ask repeatedly to hear *Snow White and the Seven Dwarfs* and to reach for Maurice Sendak's *Outside Over There, Where the Wild Things Are* and *In the Night Kitchen* over and over again?' (1984). Maurice Sendak's books, especially the *Wild Things* trilogy, have achieved this repeatable, 'classic' status. Why? Mikkelsen offers three reasons: first, the child must have reached a stage in its psychological envelopment where it can make a distinction between self and other, so it can see itself as two distinct, complementary characters in a story; second, the story needs to embody two complementary roles, usually contrasted with each other (in *Where the Wild Things Are*, Max against his mother, and later against the Wild Things). The child naturally identifies with the characters. Thirdly, the story needs to have a strong narrative structure, which's usually with pairs of opposites (good and evil, harm done and harm righted). Mikkelsen adds a fourth reason for a successful children's book: the situation/s presented in the book must relate directly to an emotional issue for the child.[3]

In many of Maurice Sendak's books, the central emotional issue is between a young child and her or his parents. In *Where the Wild Things Are*, the central conflict is an œdipal one, between Max and his mother. The Wild Things embody his escape from this conflict, his ability to imagine, but the Wild Things are also equivalents for his parents. More of this later.

III

Fairy Tales

The Grimm tales are about the pure essence of life – incest, murder, insane mothers, love, sex.

Maurice Sendak (AMS, 206)

THE MAGIC OF fairy tales continues unabated in the contemporary world, not only for children but for adults too. It is worth noting that Wilhelm and Jacob Grimms' *Children's and Household Tales* is the highest selling book in the West, after the *Bible*, since its publication in the 19th century. Of the key events in the history of the fairy and folk tale, one of the most significant must surely be the publication in 1823 of the Grimm Brothers' stories. They were translated into English by Edgar Taylor and his family, and were illustrated by George Cruikshank, one of the great illustrators of the day. It proved to be a brilliant combination of talents (we are re-publishing the original text of this ground-breaking book).

The typical fairy tale, or the fairy tale as interpreted today, is usually short (3-5 pages long), usually from a Grimm source (perhaps modified by Disney), concentrating on a character who learns how to use magic and gifts to achieve success, and often involves marriage at the end. Women are beautiful, hard-working, and passive; the men are dashing, brave, and adventurous.[1]

It's important to remember, too, that fairy tales today

usually mean a narrow range of ten to fifteen stories – always the same ones: *The Frog Prince, Snow White and the Seven Dwarfs, Cinderella, Rapunzel, Sleeping Beauty, Little Red Riding Hood, Hansel and Gretel, Beauty and the Beast, The Pied Piper, The Snow Queen, The Little Mermaid, Bluebeard, Tom Thumb, The Three Little Pigs, The Twelve Dancing Princesses, Jack and the Beanstalk, Puss In Boots,* etc.

Among the characters in wonder tales were the simple youth, Hans, Pierre, Jack, Ivan, the youngest brother or son, who seems as if he'll never do well. Then there's Cinderella, the loyal sister, the faithful bride, the clever thief, the boastful tailor, robbers, ogres, unjust kings, childless queens, princess who can't laugh; flying horses, talking fish, magic tables or sacks, a sly fox, a kind duck, nasty stepmothers, fools, greedy wolves, brave children, kindly fathers, and a beast as a bridegroom.

Literary fairy tales distinguish themselves from the oral wonder tales by allusions to religion, customs and literature, by complex or carefully constructed plots, by embellished language, and sophisticated linguistic codes.[2]

The celebrated illustrators of fairy tales include George Cruikshank, Gustave Doré, Arthur Rackham, Walter Crane, Kate Greenaway, Charles Folkard, Harry Clarke, Edmund Dulac, Klaus Ensikat, Eric Carle, Lisbeth Zwerger, Raymond Briggs, and Maurice Sendak.

According to Jack Zipes, the Grimm brothers were

> *devout Christians, industrious, moral, dedicated to their family, methodological, highly disciplined, believed in law and order based on principles of the enlightenment, cultivated their manners, speech and dress that made them acceptable among other members of the bourgeois class, and cared a great deal about maintaining the* good *name of the Grimm family.* (1988, 21).

The Grimms – Jacob Grimm (1785-1863) and Wilhem (1786-1859) – imposed a structure on fairy tales which didn't quite exist in the oral tales that were the basis for their literary interpretations. Although it seemed logical to have fairy tale heroes as industrious and cunning, aiming to improve their social status, and being rewarded for their hard work at the end of the story, it wasn't always so in oral tales.[3]

What is it about fairy tales that so fascinates readers? It is something to do with mythic, primal narratives, obviously, as studied by Vladimir Propp, C.G. Jung and post-Jungians such as Marie-Louise von Franz, Angela Carter and Emma Jung. Early books on the psychological dimension of fairy tales included Charlotte Bühler's *Das Märchen und die Phantasie des Kinders*; Sigmund Freud led the way, and Carl Jung and Géza Roheim aimed to develop Freud's theories; writers such as Marie-Louis von Franz, Emma Jung, Aneila Jaffé, Joseph Campbell, Marina Warner and Mircea Eliade analyzed fairy and folk tales from a post-Freudian and post-Jungian viewpoint; some writers (like Erich Fromm, Julius Heucher and Bruno Bettelheim) concentrated on the œdipal conflicts in the Grimm Brothers' fairy tales; and André Favat employed Charles Piaget's work on children (in *Child and the Tale*).

Fairy tales have also been the subject of semiotic, linguistic, structuralist and Marxist analyses, such as by Max Lüthi and Vladimir Propp, literary historians such as Ludwig Denecke and Heinz Rölleke, and Marxist critics such as Dieter Richter, Johannes Merkel, Carolyn Steedman, Christa Bürger, Bernard Wollenweber and Jack Zipes. Other critics have employed reader-response theory, such as Roger Sale, Hugh Crago and Aidan Chambers. Peter Hunt has developed 'childist' criticism, while Eleanor Cameron has been sceptical of many forms of criticism.[4]

So compelling have fairy tales been that almost all important Germanic writers from the mid-19th century onward have attempted to write them: Rainer Maria Rilke, Franz Kafka, Thomas Mann, Bertholt Brecht, Theodor Storm, Gottfried Keller, Hermann Hesse, Carl Zuckmayer, Gerhart Hauptmann, Alfred Döblin, Georg Kaiser, Kurt Tucholky, Walter Hasenclever, Joachim Ringelnatz, Kurt Schwitters, Hans Fallada,

Oskar Maria Graf, Erich Kästner, Siegfried Lenz, Helmut Heißenbüttel, Ingeborg Bachmann, Peter Hacks, Günther Kunert, Christa Wolf, Irmtraud Morgner, Peter Härtling, Max Frisch, Nicolas Born, Peter Handke and Günter Grass (J. Zipes, 1989, 86).

For Angela Carter, fairy tales are part of folklore, not 'high art', which comes from the proletariat, not the bourgeoisie; in Carter's proto-feminist view, fairy tales speak of spirited, resourceful women, a female character who is 'clever, or brave, or good, or silly, or cruel, or sinister, or awesomely unfortunate' (xiii). Some fairy tales – those of the Grimms and Charles Perrault for example – sometimes punish desire and wildness. In *Little Red Riding Hood*, the protagonist is told not to be adventurous, not to talk to strangers, not to wander from the path. In the work of the Grimms, Hans Christian Andersen and Perrault, one sees the mechanisms of control in a patriarchal world at work – the urge to police desire and adventure, independent thinking and self-liberation. The forbidden is suppressed. Taboos are skirted around, or tackled, unleashing violence and retribution. French feminist Luce Irigaray said in *This Sex Which Is Not One*: 'what is most strictly forbidden to women today is that they should attempt to express their own pleasure' (1991, 125).

LITTLE RED RIDING HOOD AND *WHERE THE WILD THINGS ARE*

JACK ZIPES IS one of the very best contemporary commentators on fairy tales, on a par with any of the celebrated critics, such as Bruno Bettelheim, Marie-Louise van Franz or the Grimms themselves. If you want an excellent introduction to fairy tales, you can't do better than reading Jack Zipes. Zipes, in *Fairy Tales and the Art of Subversion: The Classical Genre for Children and the Process of Civilization*, sees *Little Red*

Riding Hood as a patriarchal tale of male power, where a young woman is initiated into the masculinist social world via a rape fantasy (1983). For Zipes, there's a 'Little Red Riding Hood syndrome' in Western culture which perverted sexuality in the 18th and 19th centuries and led to 'an instrumentalization of the body', so that (*pace* Michel Foucault) sexuality became a part of the 'development of bio-politics to bring about the supervision of the body as a machine for maximum use and profit'.[5]

For Jack Zipes, the folk tale was originally an oral narrative form that made sense of life for 'common', working class people. It was not a literary form, but a reflection of their needs and aspirations; it reflected their perception of the moral and social order of the time (1979, 5). In *Don't Bet on the Prince: Contemporary Feminist Fairy Tales in North America and England,* Zipes reckoned that Charles Perrault and the Grimm Brothers had appropriated oral and folk tales and turned them into 'male-cultivated' literary versions (1986, 227).[6] According to Zipes, Perrault made some important changes to the folk tale of *Little Red Riding Hood* when he revised it in 1697: the protagonist became 'spoiled, negligent, and naïve'; she is dressed now in red, colour of sin in Christianity; she speaks to and makes a compact with the wolf; she does pretty much what the wolf wants, and is not clever enough to outwit him.

Wolfishness is associated with sensuality, nature, baseness, animality; the wolf is demonized in the West, becomes associated with the Devil, with witchcraft (lycanthropy), all things 'other' and unknown. The wolf is the sinful 'wild side' of human nature, always to be suppressed; the wolf symbolizes a fear of intercourse and conception (C.G. Jung), or (female) wildness (Sigmund Freud), or racial inferiority (racist German folklorists), depending on which authority one employs.[7]

Maurice Sendak's most famous book, *Where the Wild Things Are* is also about a child encountering something potentially monstrous. Rather than using wolves (though a wolfish image does appear on the wall of Max's house, and he wears his wolf-suit), Sendak went for half-jokey, half-scary monsters.[8] In both *Little Red Riding Hood* and *Where the Wild Things Are* a child ventures forth from the domestic, maternal environment into the wide world (both move from a house to a wild forest). In both tales, the relationship with the mother is pivotal: the mother and her maternal power bring back and re-centre the child. In *Where the Wild Things Are* and *Little Red Riding Hood* the power of the mother in righting the world is embodied in the promise of good food. At the end of *Little Red Riding Hood* the emphasis shifts from being eaten and pulled out of the wolf's belly to the mother again providing food and wine for the grandmother in Little Red Cap's next trip into the now-secure forest. At the end of *Where the Wild Things Are* it is Max's desire to be loved (maternally) that makes him (wish to) return to his home.

Though the mother does not appear in any picture in *Where the Wild Things Are,* her presence is huge. She represents everything that Max rebels against, and, of course, everything that he pines for in the Land of the Wild Things. The differences between *Where the Wild Things Are* and *Little Red Riding Hood* include the sexual element: in *Little Red Riding Hood* the gender of the girl and the wolf is significant: the wolf stands for, unsubtly, the strange men mothers warn their children about. In *Where the Wild Things Are*, however, Max is definitely prepubescent and there is nothing carnal about his relations with the Wild Things. The Wild Things themselves are also sexless, of indeterminate gender.

MOTHER GOOSE

YOU DON'T KNOW WHO the teller is in the fairy tale. For feminists, fairy tales come from a common ground of primal maternity, a mythic female space embodied by that shadowy but powerful figure, 'Mother Goose', called 'Ma Mère l'Oie' in French, 'an old woman [of either sex] sitting by the fireside, spinning – literally 'spinning a yarn'' (A. Carter, x).

Maurice Sendak wrote a piece on the figure of Mother Goose in the *Sunday Herald Tribune* (Hallowe'en, 1965). Sendak notes that *Mother Goose* or 'nursery' rhymes were made more for adults than for children (C, 12). Sendak enjoys the 'earthy, ambiguous, double-entendre quality of so many of the verses' (C, 12). His own pictures have that strange, haunting quality of *Mother Goose/* nursery rhymes. The 'elusive, mythic and mysterious elements' (C, 14) of *Mother Goose* rhymes are what fascinate Sendak: it is these elements which transcend the notion of 'nonsense' in *Mother Goose* rhymes. Sendak dislikes too sentimental or lightweight versions of the rhymes. British illustrator Kate Greenaway, Sendak felt, had provided the wrong sort of interpretation of nursery rhymes (in her illustrations for *Mother Goose*, 1881). Greenaway was delicate but antiseptic (C, 17). Much more to Sendak's taste was Randolph Caldecott with his 'syncopated' versions of *Hey Diddle Diddle* and *Baby Bunting,* which melded words and pictures in a new way.

FAIRY TALES AS FANTASY

FOR MAURICE SENDAK, fairy tales contain fundamental truths about humanity. Just because they're 'fantasy' does not invalidate them as works of art, works of insight and truth. Fairy tales are not 'realistic', they are 'symbolic poetry', suggests Max Lüthi in *Once Upon a Time: On the Nature of*

Fairy Tales (1976, 66). Fantasy is, for Sendak, as for many writers, simply a different form of realism. The painter Wassily Kandinsky said that abstraction equalled realism, that abstraction is a form of realism. The sculptor Constantin Brancusi too was annoyed when critics called his work 'abstract'. What do they mean? he asked, my work is actually realist. Thus, for Sendak, as for writers and psychoanalysts such as Joseph Campbell, Mircea Eliade, Carl Jung, Angela Carter and Sara Maitland, fantasy and fairy tales offer a form of 'reality' or insight that traditional forms of 'realism' or 'naturalism' cannot produce. Indeed, for these writers and thinkers, there is no distinct boundary between reality and fantasy. While severely 'rational' figures such as politicians cannot use the discourse of fantasy, because no one would believe they could ever get things done, writers such as Maurice Sendak, Ursula Le Guin, Tanith Lee, Margaret Atwood, J.G. Ballard and Michael Moorcock know and value fantasy and fairy tales.

For Maurice Sendak, the use of the imagination and fantasy is essential in being alive.[9] Sendak regards a 'factual' book as imaginative as a fantasy book (C, 72). Sendak on childhood:

> *Childhood is a difficult time.* (C, 152)
> *Children do live in fantasy and reality, in a way we no longer remember. They have a cool sense of the logic of illogic, and they shift very easily from one sphere to another. Fantasy is the core of all writing for children, as I think it is for the writing of any book, for any creative act, perhaps for the act of living.* (C, 174)
> *Children do live in both fantasy and reality; they move back and forth with ease, in a way that we no longer remember how to do.* (AMS, 65)

Maurice Sendak believes that children can handle a lot more than adults reckon. For Sendak, children's books are too heavily policed by adults, and don't need to be. Adults, he claims, are too anxious about what children consume. 'Children are much more catholic in taste; will tolerate ambiguities, peculiarities, and things illogical' (C, 192). Sendak wants a liberal approach to children's illustration. He wants to be able to work unfettered by censors who police his efforts. As he puts it, '[t]he artist has to be a little bit bewildering and a little bit wild and a little bit disorderly.' (C, 192)

THE BLOODY CHAMBER: CENSORSHIP, VIOLENCE AND FAIRY TALES

MAURICE SENDAK ABHORS in particular the censorship of fairy tales. He dislikes those collections of fairy tales that bowdlerize the stories for children. He disdains the fact that the original fairy tales are distorted because of censorship.[10]

> *Clearly the brothers Grimm and Mr H.C. Andersen never bothered their heads about providing so-called healthy or suitable literature for children* [remarked Sendak]. *How fortunate for us they were only interested in telling a good story! And they are stories charged with originality and a tremendous understanding of the fascinating tangle of life...* (C, 158)

Fairy tales are violent, difficult, ambiguous, erotic, as well as charming, sweet, sentimental and lyrical. But fairy tales were never intended for children: they were always produced by and for adults; only in the later part of the 19th century did the shift towards catering for children occur.

Publishers, teachers, educational boards, broadcasters and filmmakers have all censored fairy tales at one time or another. In *Hansel and Gretel* the witch is pushed into an oven; in *Cinderella* the sisters' eyes are pecked out; in *Little Red Riding Hood* the wolf eats two women; and the witch is made to dance in red-hot shoes in *Snow White*.

The violence in fairy tales immediately makes them suspect food for children, who, it is claimed by media pundits, rightwing religious fundamentalists and media watchdogs, copy what they consume in the media. Children, it is claimed, have copied the antics of cartoon characters. If cartoons are violent, then children can become violent.

It is this simplistic argument, this puritanical need to protect children that writers such as Maurice Sendak detest. It is this form of censorship and policing that destroys works of art. The opposers of censorship are those of the liberal camp, advocating the sovereignty of notions such as self-expression, and the rights of free speech. It's not so much a question of being right or left wing, republican or democrat, but of minimising the mechanisms and institutions of oppression. What the liberal artist doesn't want is someone saying you can do this but not that. The liberal artist must imagine s/he is beyond the dictates of this or that regime or set of laws. S/he must think s/he is free to express themselves as s/he will. (The writers of *The Simpsons* have relentlessly attacked rightwing do-gooders in many episodes, in particular about cartoon violence. *The Simpsons* has also brilliantly sent up Maurice Sendak and *Where the Wild Things Are* in an incisive parody).

It is significant, then, that when Maurice Sendak and Lore Segal chose the stories from the Grimms to put into *The Juniper Tree and Other Tales From Grimm,* they should keep in the violence. Of the Grimm stories they selected, Sendak remarked:

> *They have absolutely everything: magic, wish-fulfilment, bloodcurdling horror, consuming passion – the works. The material is remarkably rich and deep, like good soil.* (AMS, 192)

In fact, it is collections such as Maurice Sendak's, which do not edit or soften the stories, that reminds one of the visceral nature of the fairy tales. There is, for instance, much spilling of blood in the stories. Fairy and folk stories were not intended to be bloodless. Myths have always had blood spilt in them, and many deaths. Death is part of the overall emotional, spiritual and psychological impact of world mythologies. To erase or soften death in mythology destroys their meaning. When one reads Sendak's *The Juniper Tree and Other Tales From Grimm,* then, or read the Brothers Grimm uncensored, one is struck by the violence of the stories, not because the violence is troubling, but because many other versions of fairy and folk tales produced for adults or for children are carefully edited. The reader coming to Maurice Sendak via *In the Night Kitchen* might not be prepared for the sight of the bloody basin full of hacked limbs in *Fitcher's Feathered Bird* in *The Juniper Tree and Other Tales From Grimm*:

> *She put it in the keyhole and she just turned it a very little but the door sprang open. And what did she see? In the middle of the room there was a great bloody basin full of dead people hacked into pieces, and next to it stood a butcher's block with a gleaming ax on it.* (JT, 72-73)

Like many commentators, J.R.R. Tolkien was against the evisceration of fairy tales, taking the violent, horror and other elements out which would make them untroubling for children. That was a kind of literary vandalism which wrecked the original stories. Tolkien spoke lovingly of tales such as *The Juniper Tree* and confessed:

> *I do not think I was harmed by the horror in* the fairy-tale setting, *out of whatever dark beliefs and practices of the past it may have come. Such stories have now a mythical or total (unanalysable) effect, and effect quite independent of the findings of Comparative Folk-lore, and one which it cannot spoil or explain; they open a door on Other Time, and if we pass through, though only for a moment, we stand outside our own time, outside Time itself, maybe.* (1983, 128-9)

For J.R.R. Tolkien, it was ultimately more dangerous to bowdlerize fairy tales than to present them as they were before editors and critics got hold of them. As to the rewrites and imitations of fairy tales, they could be 'merely silly', or patronizing, or 'covertly sniggering', winking at the adult audience (1983, 136).

✪

Lurking behind every fairy tale is the 'bloody' or 'forbidden chamber', a dark underworld of raw feeling and spiritual power. Behind every fairy tale is the bloody chamber of *Bluebeard,* a place that is at once taboo and fascinating, a place that is both hidden and aching to be revealed (variants in Grimms' tales include *The Robber's Bridegroom* and *Fitcher's Feather Bird*). The temptation story usually involves a woman opening the forbidden chamber, related to the ancient myths of Pandora (and Pandora's box), Psyche, and Orpheus. The bloody chamber is desired and feared. It is a place of love and death.

As Sigmund Freud knew well, taboos contain really powerful things. That's why they're taboos. Fairy tales continually present readers with taboos and thresholds: the taboos and thresholds have to be dealt with by the protagonist in the tale. The moralistic aspect of fairy tales is direct: either the protagonist opens the door or doesn't: there is no equivocation, one must choose correctly. The wrong choice is always swiftly punished. The exoteric choices reflect esoteric or inner developments. Sometimes the price to pay for passing a threshold is death, as the women die in *Bluebeard* who cannot resist unlocking the door to the forbidden chamber. Sometimes there is an extraordinary, miraculous reward for the right kind of endeavour.

Fairy tales such as *Hansel and Gretel* are actually about child abuse – the sort of severe child abuse that leads to death. *Hansel and Gretel* opens, like a crime or detective story, with the threat of death. Two sorts of death are evoked: either the children die, or the whole family dies. This is the stepmother's thinking. The opening of *Hansel and Gretel* is bowlderized in children's illustrated books. References to death and coffins are left out. But they are a key part of the horror of the story:

> *"Oh, you fool!" said she. "Then all four of us will starve to death – you may as well start planing the planks for our coffins," and she gave him no peace until he agreed.* (JT, 153)

The fairy tale *The Story of One Who Set Out To Study Fear* is full of death, the very stench of death. It is about the search for full consciousness of life, which, in the grand old European tradition (William Shakespeare, Marquis de Sade, Charles Baudelaire, Johann Wolfgang von Goethe, Arthurian romance) means confronting death up close. The story is rich in gallows humour, as the youth dives into the nightmare underworld of life. *The Story of One Who Set Out To Study Fear* is one of the more macabre of Grimms' *Children's and Household Tales*, a quality which probably attracted Maurice Sendak. *The Story of One Who Set Out To Study Fear* moves, finally from death to sex, and ends with a sexual experience.

> *Her maid said, "I know what to do. His flesh is going to learn all about creeping." She went out to the brook that flowed full of minnows. At night, when the young king was asleep, his wife had to pull off the covers and pour the bucketful of cold water and the minnows on him. The little fish squirmed all over him, and he woke up and cried, "Sometimes is making my flesh creep! Dear wife, how my flesh is creeping! Ah, now I know what it's like when one's flesh creeps."* (JT, 41)

The appearance of the figure of death in the bell tower, which Maurice Sendak chooses as the moment to illustrate from *The Story of One Who Set Out To Study Fear*, is the archetypal ghost or death, familiar from mediæval paintings, and Ingmar Bergman's *The Seventh Seal*. Sendak's scene from *The Story of One Who Set Out To Study Fear* is wholly *mittel* European, wholly in keeping with the Germanic historical tradition of the Grimm Brothers' world.

WISHING

THEN THERE'S WISHING. The three wishes in fairy tales is at once infinite desire and infinite prohibition. Wishing trades on the immortal question 'what if...?' *What if* one had a million dollars... *what if* one was incredibly beautiful... *what if* one had unlimited food? In fairy tale wishing, infinite desire is unleashed: the implication is that *you can have anything!* But everyone knows, even very young children, that this is not true. The world is finite – the energy, food supply, money or beauty must come from somewhere. Always with the wishes come limits, laws, problems. As soon as the starving mother and daughter are given their magic porridge pot by the witch, it goes wrong. The mother is too greedy: greed and selfishness is punished in fairy tales. Much as one would like the wisher to choose the ultimate wish: *I wish for an infinite number of subsequent wishes!* it never works that way. The eager, grasping ego loses out, eventually, to the humble, poor chooser and wisher. Compassion and altruism win out over greed and unkindness. Wishing is dangerous: all too easily characters are too impatient, and wish for the wrong thing, and their nose starts growing, or the black pudding is stuck to it (in Charles Perrault's *The Three Wishes*). The moral of that story seems to be that you should appreciate what you already have and where you really are. Wishing for other things, like money, or being a king or queen, won't solve anything, won't make you happier. In *The Three Wishes*, the poor woodcutter finally wishes to have wife back to normal (even though he thinks that the sausage on her nose isn't too bad an addition).

Maurice Sendak does not use the ritual of wishing that much in his own stories, though he did include the most arrogant story of wishing in his selection of Grimms' stories, *The Fisherman and His Wife,* where the woman wishes to be Pope, then Emperor, then God, at which point, of course, she reverts to being a poor fisherman's wife again.

WONDER

THE SENSE OF *WONDER* is one of the essential ingredients that sets the oral wonder tale apart from its oral companions, the folk tale, the chronicle, the anecdote, the myth, the legend and the fable. As Jack Zipes puts it:

> *Wonder causes astonishment, and the marvellous object or phenomenon is often regarded as a supernatural occurrence and can be an omen or portent. It gives rise to admiration, fear, awe, and reverence. In the oral wonder tale, listeners are to ponder about the workings of the universe where anything can happen at any time, and these happy or fortuitous events are never to be explained.* (2000, xviii)

Magical objects in fairy tales include seven league boots, porridge pots, caps that fire cannons, mirrors that talk, tablecloths that provide food, swords and clubs, and invisible capes and clothes.

SHAPE-SHIFTING

MAURICE SENDAK EMPLOYS many examples of shape-shifting in his stories, as one might expect from such a dynamic illustrator (and transformation is absolutely central to film animation, which Sendak draws on). The figure of the shape-changer is very ancient: the archaic shaman is the model for all deities, magicians, animals and witches who can transform themselves. In Sendak's fairy tales, characters turn themselves either deliberately or unconsciously: in his *Wild Things* trilogy, Max puts on his wolf-suit, just like a primitive witch doctor, Ida wears the yellow rain cape and flies, like a magician, while Mickey, more practical, pounds and punches cooking batter into an aeroplane.

Wonder tales, oral tales which pre-date literary fairy tales, have *transformation* as one of their foundations, in particular miraculous transformation. As Jack Zipes noted, '[e]verybody and everything can be transformed in a wonder tale'. Usually there was the transformation of the social status of the protagonists (2000, xvii).

Traditionally, shape-shifting means moving from one ontological plane to another: from boy to bird means moving higher up, into transcendence of earthly matters. Being turned by a witch into a frog is clearly a regression to a lower level. The frog is like a primitive, miniature, even caricature version of a human being. For Marie-Louise von Franz the frog as the embodiment of the unconscious is usually aiming to become conscious: it wants to become conscious (M. Franz, 1980, 70).

Maurice Sendak does not usually employ the regressive form of shape-shifting: his fairy tales (certainly the *Wild Things* trilogy) are about protagonists who are definitely on the way up. They are feisty, resourceful types, who transform themselves, via a combination of circumstance, desire, intelligence, wit, courage and luck.

THE DARK FOREST

THE DARK FOREST of fairy tales is the place of initiation and trial. It lies on the edge of the familiar, everyday world of the fairy tale. It is where the protagonist gets lost, meets strange creatures, undergoes transformations and spells. It is, typically, one of the first places the protagonist enters on the journey outwards from the home, in *Snow White and the Seven Dwarfs, Little Red Riding Hood* or *Hansel and Gretel* for example.

At the end of *Little Red Riding Hood*, in the Grimms' version, the protagonist learns the moral lesson of straying from the straight and narrow path: '[n]ever again will you stray from the path by yourself and go into the forest when your mother has forbidden it' (J. Grimm, 104).

The forest is a zone of otherness, strangeness, enchantment and the unknown. In (Jungian) psychological terms, it is the unconscious, or confusion, a realm of instability, a *regressus ad uterum*, a place of re-creation and rebirth, where the ego/ soul/ heroine is tested and initiated. The enchanted or dark forest is a place of wild things, such as dragons in caves, or witches in their gloomy houses; it is also a place of death (and dragons, witches, caves and darkness are linked with death or the 'dark side' of life).

As Jack Zipes notes, no one controls the dark forest, though it may control you. It represents something wilder, stranger, darker and more mysterious than any individual; the natural world, a plenitude that can be life-giving as well as threatening or death-dealing.

Jacob and Wilhelm Grimm, in their *Children's and Household Tales*, expressed some of the Germanic love of forests, which is fuelled by awe and mysticism. There are clichés that abound about the Germanic mystification of forests as places of ritual and magic, sites of notions of community, race and origins. However, these clichés about the dark forest do form much of the background of fairy tales, in the Grimms' books especially.

Maurice Sendak employs no less than three 'dark forest' motifs in *Where the Wild Things Are*: first is the traditional enchanted forest, then the ocean, over which Max sails for a year and a day, and then the land of the Wild Things itself.

Max doesn't slay the monsters, but he does, like a mythic hero, become master of them (the mastery is vital – and not only because Max is a young child, it applies to any hero; *Where the Wild Things Are* follows classical mythological structures). In *Outside Over There*, Ida has to travel to the goblins' underground caves, a classic fairy tale setting (recalling, for example, the underground rooms in Hans Christian Andersen's *The Tinder Box*). To emphasize the rebirth image, after Ida has made the goblins dance into a steam, Sendak has Ida's sister appear in an egg-shell. The child's journey into the dark forest in *Dear Mili* is altogether more troubling: giant hawks and black crows screech in a scene full of foreboding.

ILLUSTRATIONS

Some classic fairy tale illustrations

1. Anonymous illustration for *Sleeping Beauty*, 1900.
2. Kate Greenaway (coloured by Kronheim), 1869.
3. Arthur Rackham's illustration to the Grimms' *Rumpelstiltskin*, 1910.
4. Two Arthur Hughes' illustrations for George MacDonald, 1874.
5. George Cruikshank's illustrations to *Cinderella*, 1854.
6. Classic Gustave Doré fairy tale illustrations, to Charles Perrault, 1867, including *Puss In Boots*, and *Little Red Riding Hood*.

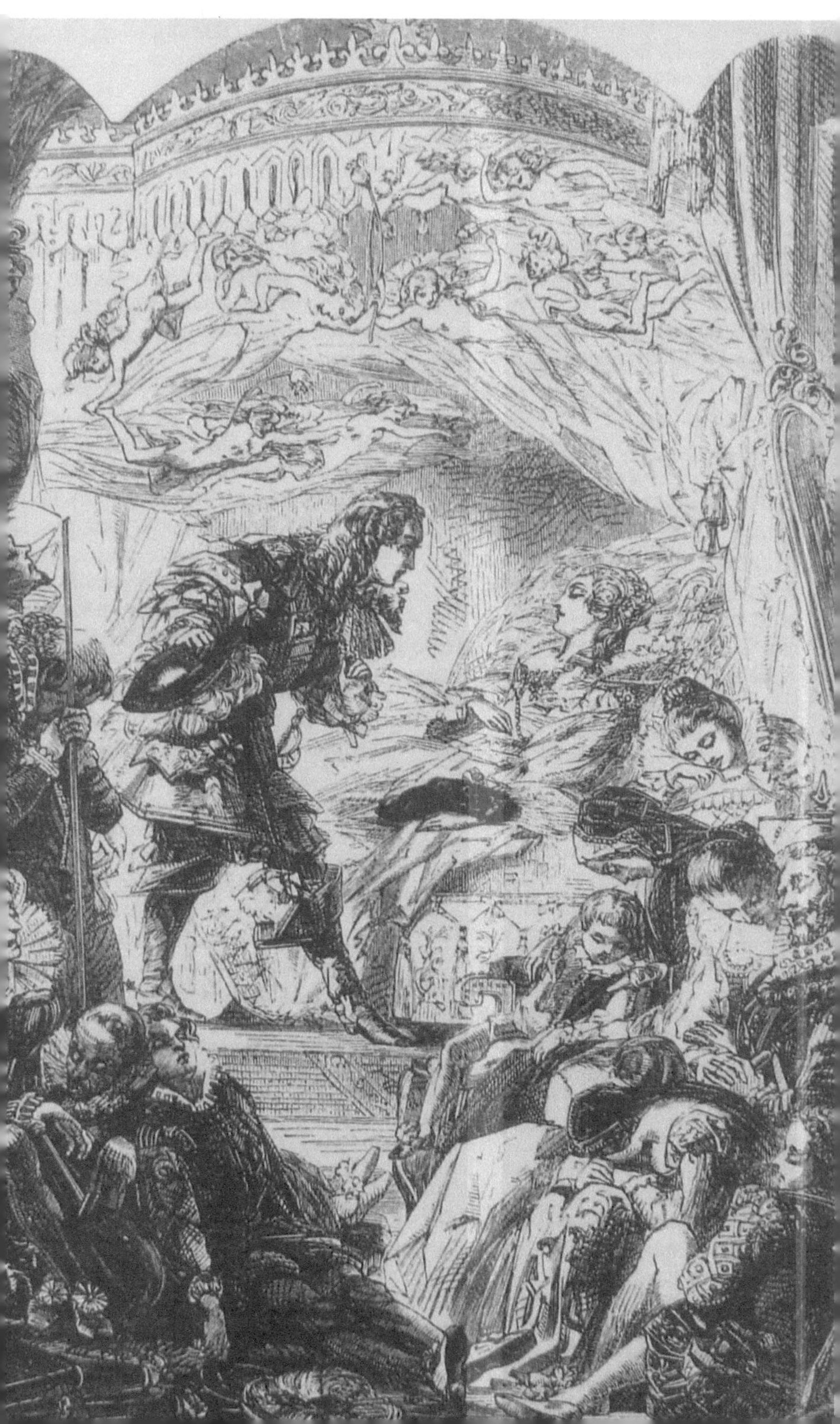

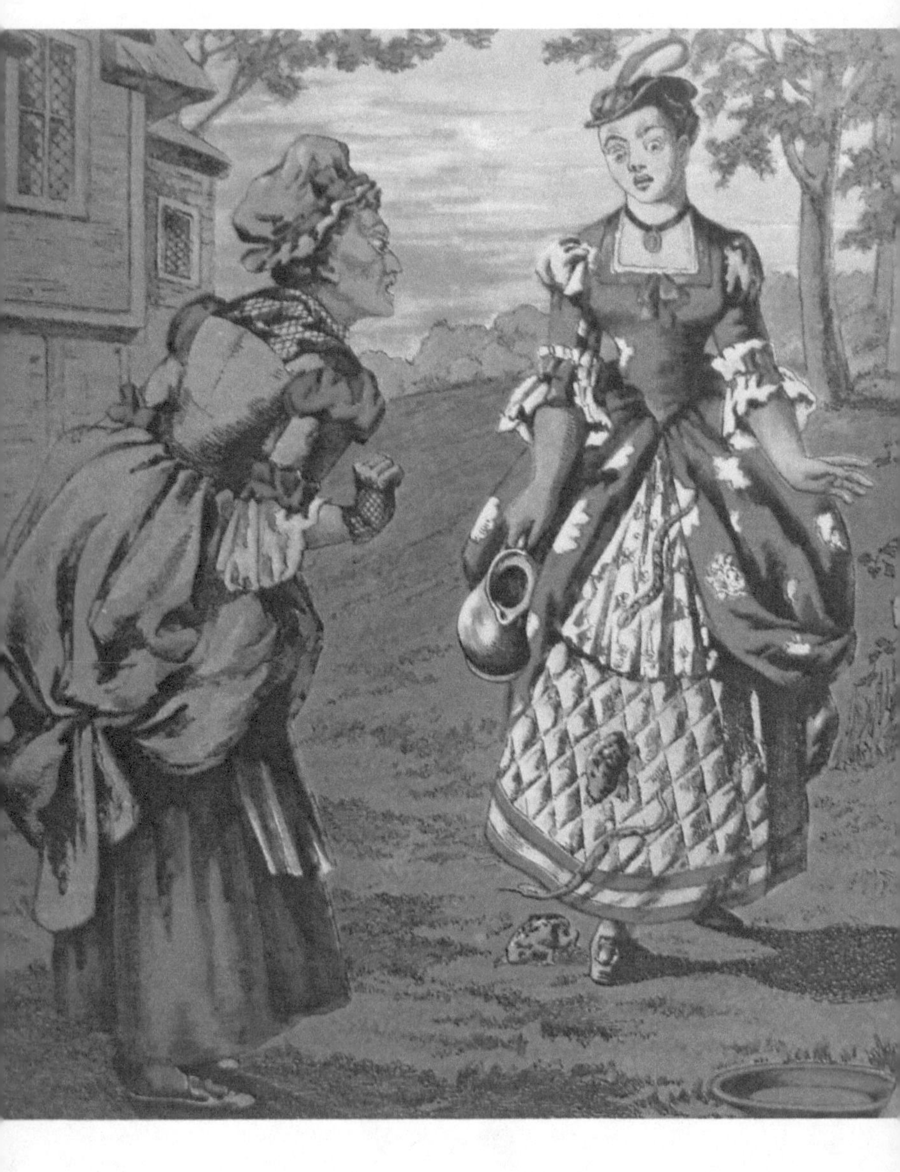

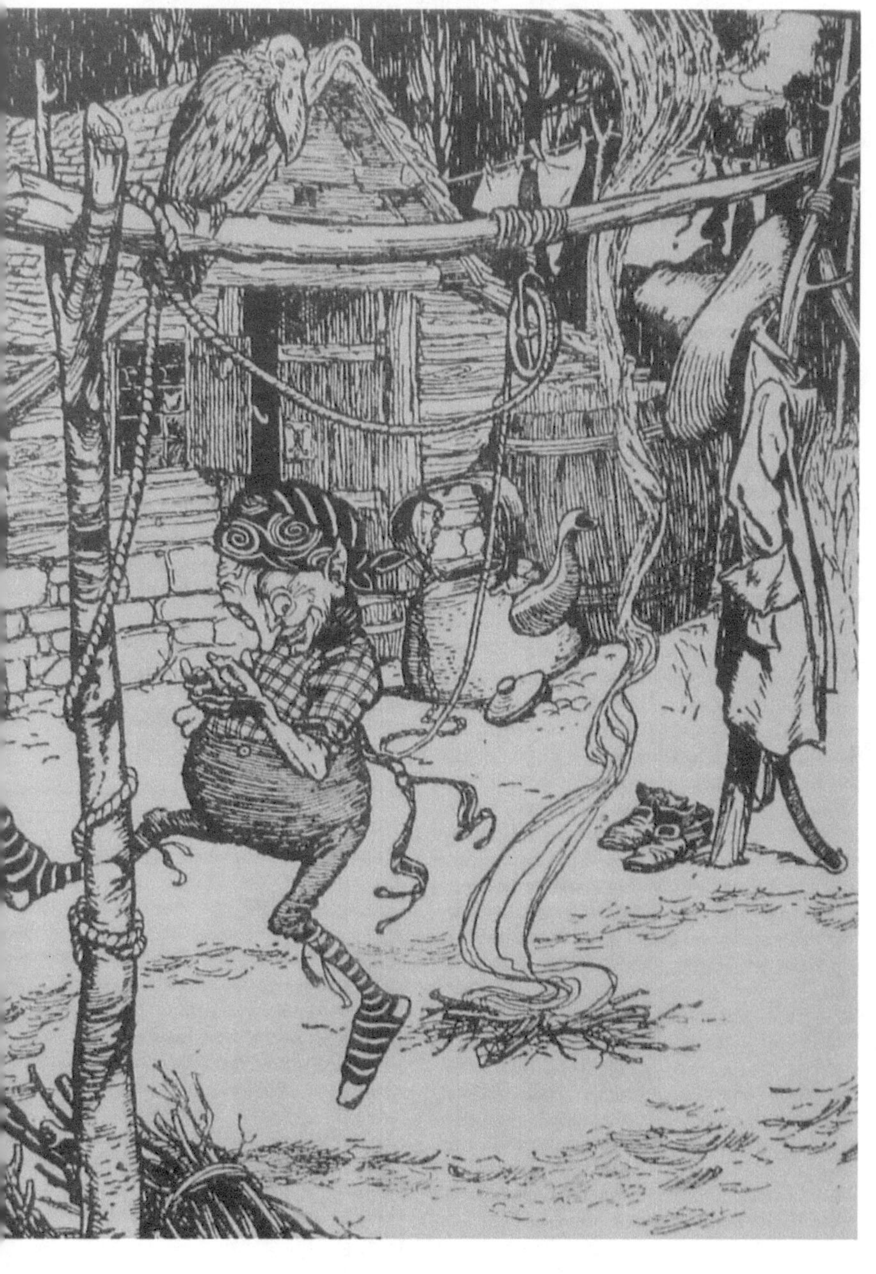

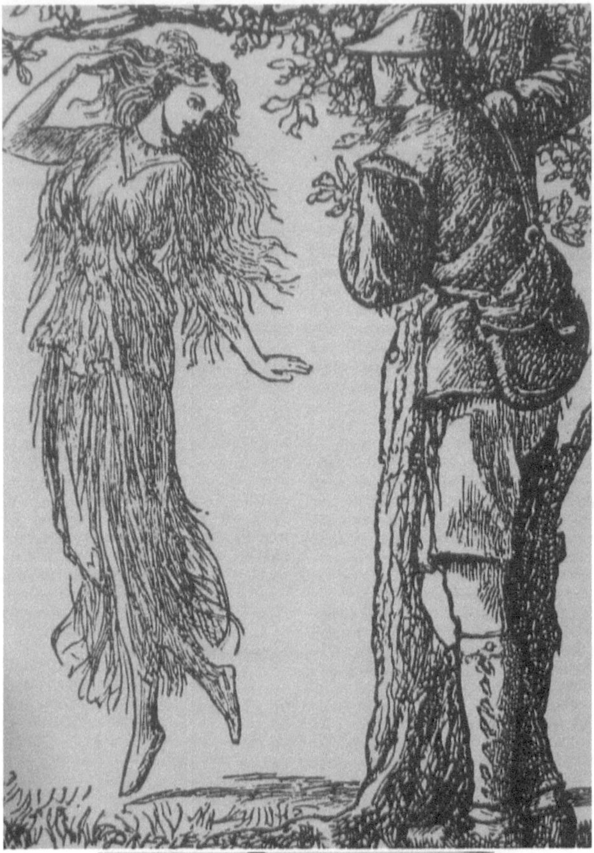

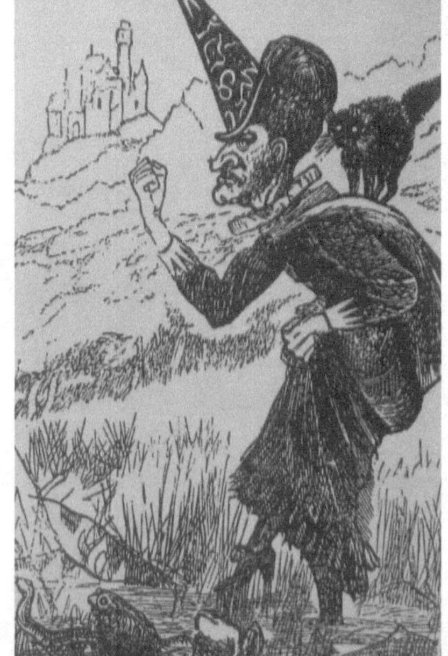

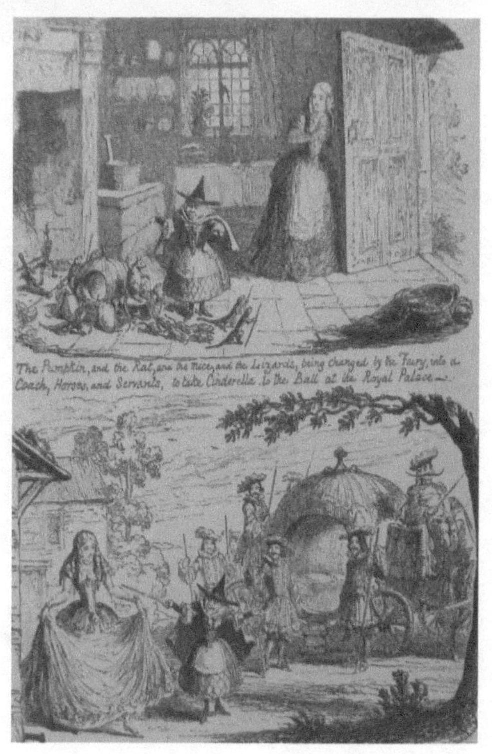
The Pumpkin, and the Rat, and the Mice, and the Lizards, being changed by the Fairy, into a
Coach, Horses, and Servants, to take Cinderella to the Ball at the Royal Palace

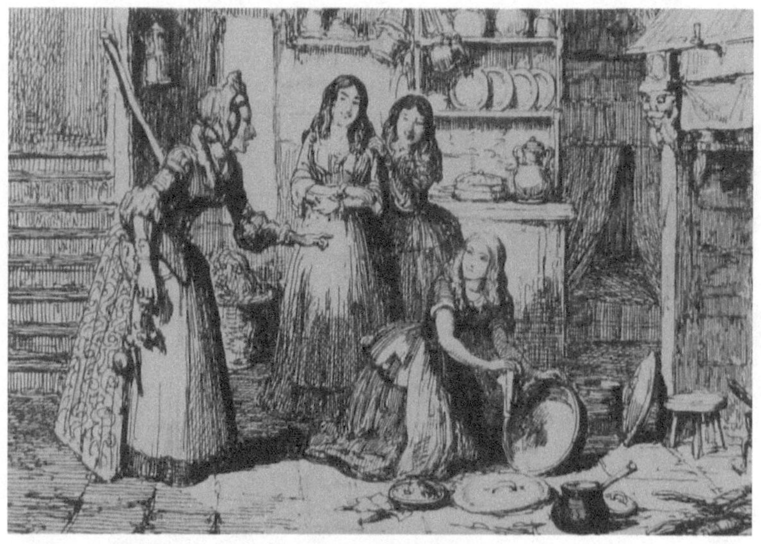

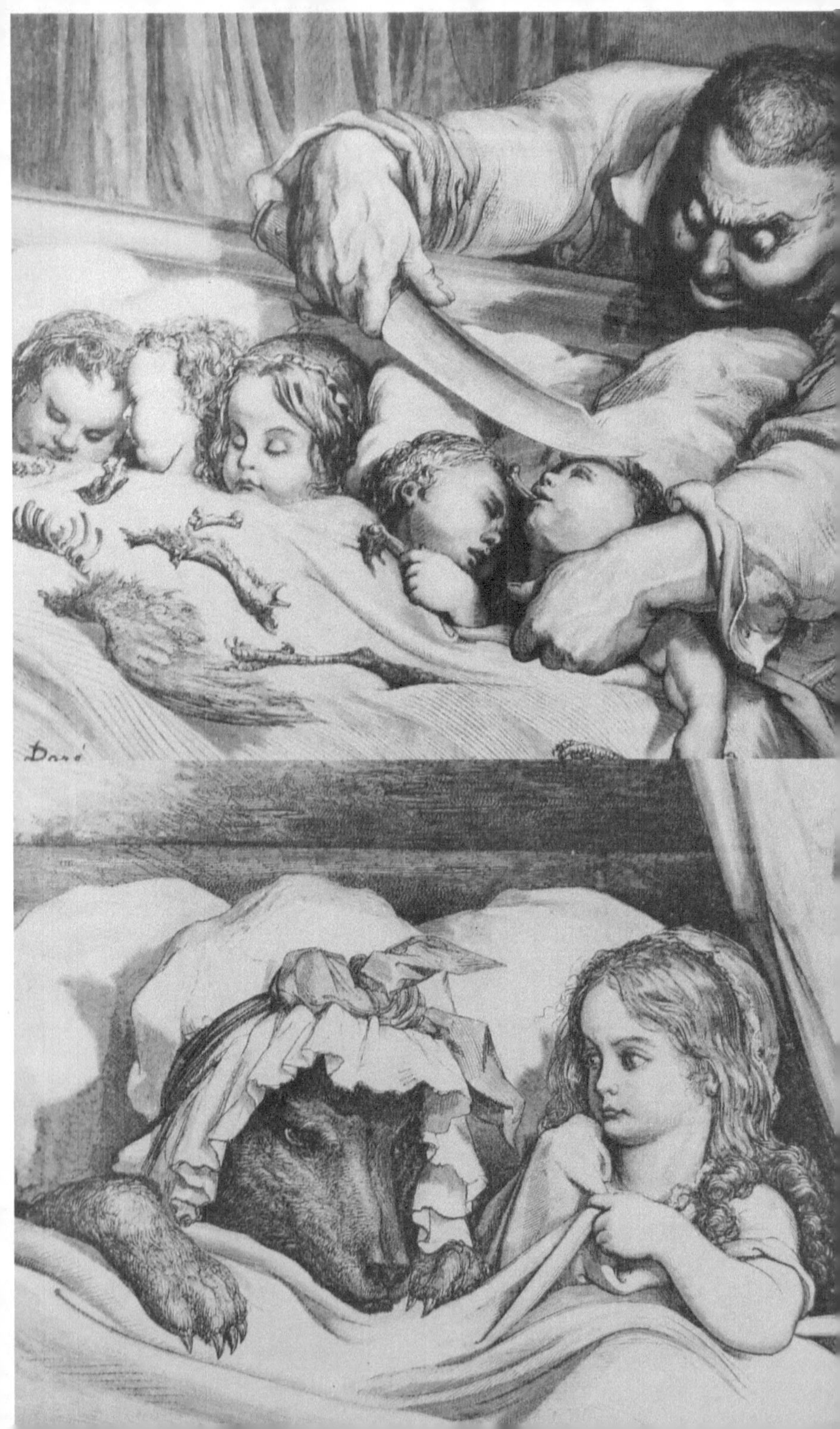

IV

Sendak and Grimm: The Juniper Tree

THE GRIMM BROTHERS – Wilhelm (1786-1859) and Jakob (1785-1863) – tower over fairy tale culture. Maurice Sendak's 1973 book *The Juniper Tree and Other Tales From Grimm* is an attempt to give back to the traditional fairy tale some of the darkness and power it used to possess. What is to be avoided, and what Sendak loathes, is the dressing up of fairy tales in sweetness and light. This is what happens in Walt Disney's movies, and in Hollywood versions of fairy tales (think of the 1958 George Pal *Tom Thumb*, or Danny Kaye cavorting about as the all-singing all-dancing Hans Christian Andersen in Sam Goldwyn's 1952 movie). It is characteristic of Sendak, for instance, that *Pinocchio* should be his favourite Disney feature film, being the most disturbing of the Disney features (the scenes at Pleasure Island, where Pinocchio, Lampwick and their chums are turned into donkeys, are very creepy).

In his piece on Hans Christian Andersen (1966),[1] Maurice Sendak noted that the fairy tale form enabled Andersen to loosen up with his writing (C, 30). Before he re-read Andersen, Sendak regarded him as inferior to Grimm, 'a sentimental, pious, sadistic man' (C, 31). Sendak was pleasantly surprised to find Andersen much better than he had thought, and he came to admire Andersen's storytelling talents. Even so, Andersen could still be bad: '[a]t his worst, he dreadfully sentimentalizes children; they rarely have the spunk, shrewdness, and character with which he endows his inanimate objects.' (C, 33)

Only when one surveys children's picture book illustrations of the past does one realize how saccharine is 20th century illustration for children. In W. Tomlinson's drawing of the moment in *Little Red Riding Hood* when the wolf gets his comeuppance we see quite plainly two men wielding an axe and a long knife. This wolf is going to die bloodily. Although the illustration (*c.* 1880) isn't particularly good, the illustrator doesn't shy away from the fact of the wolf's death. The moment of death is very rarely depicted in children's picture books. Maurice Sendak himself does not show death scenes: rather, he often chooses moments of stasis before or after action, or one scene which sums up more than one moment from the fairy tale.

✪

Fairy tales are of course a gift to illustrators, and to film-makers. Some of the great children's illustrators have tackled fairy tales. Indeed, how can one resist? It is not surprising that Maurice Sendak should find illustrating Grimms' fairy tales such a difficult task, for he regards the Grimms' works so highly. Illustrating *Where the Wild Things Are*, Sendak says, was the end of a long apprenticeship (C, 154), but the culmination of his work in children's book illustration is *The Juniper Tree and Other Tales From Grimm.*[2] Sendak knew that his illustrations for Grimm had to be absolutely, completely, utterly *right.* No half-measures, nothing slapdash, nothing sloppy.

Maurice Sendak's pictures for *The Juniper Tree and Other Tales From Grimm* are highly compressed.[3] He has squashed a lot of information into each picture. Sendak employs Renaissance space, but condenses it and flattens it. Objects in the distance are brought close to the picture plane. Volume is evoked with the dark shading and crosshatching which has been a part of Sendak's illustration style from *Where the Wild Things Are* onwards (and is such a key element in Jasper Johns' art, for instance). Sendak's sense of space recalls not the Italian Renaissance but the Northern European Renaissance painters, in particular the art of Konrad Witz, Hans Memling, Hieronymous Bosch, Quentin Massys, Rogier van der Weyden and Jan van Eyck.

Maurice Sendak has clearly learnt his lesson from European forms of illustration, and not just from book illustrators of the 18th and 19th centuries. His Grimm illustrations evoke the sense of darkness, intensity, brooding melancholy and compressed space that one finds in Albrecht Dürer's woodcuts or Rogier van der Weyden's altarpieces. Visiting Europe (on a research trip for the Grimm book), Sendak was deeply moved by seeing Dürer's art in the flesh, and Albrecht Altdorfer, and Mathias Grünewald's incredibly searing *Isenheim Altarpiece* (1515, Colmar). He visited the Grimm Museum in Kassel. In 1953, Sendak visited Paris for the first time, and was bowled over by the Louvre:

> *There they all were, the real thing – Titians, Da Vincis, Raphaels! paintings I had always read about and maybe even seen reproduced, but they were right in front of me.* (AMS, 51)

As Friedrich Nietzsche put it, Paris is absolutely the city for an artist. The illustrators of the Grimms that Maurice Sendak rated the highest were George Cruikshank, Ludwig Grimm and Otto Ubbelohde (AMS, 197).

Some of Maurice Sendak's Grimm pictures directly evoke moments in the history of art, such as the illustration for *The Devil and His Three Golden Hairs* (which was based on the portrait of Katherina Viehmann, as used for the frontispiece of Ludwig Grimm's second edition of the tales. She is one of the archetypal images of an old storyteller, a Germanic 'Mother Goose'). The woman holds the Devil in her lap. 'It is a highly erotic and disturbingly ambiguous drawing, with the Devil lying awkwardly and suggestively in the old woman's lap', said Sendak (AMS, 200).

The most obvious model for this image of a young man

lying in an old woman's lap is that of Jesus after the Crucifixion in the lap of the Virgin Mary. It's the *Pietà* image, celebrated in so many Renaissance paintings, the flight of the alienated outsider male back to his mother. The image of the son lying in the primal embrace of the mother is older than Christianity, of course: there's Isis and Osiris and Tammuz and Ishtar in ancient Sumerian and Egyptian religion.

Maurice Sendak's illustration to *The Master Thief* chooses a moment when sex, death and violence converge. It shows a corpse at a window being shot by the count; next to him is his naked wife, looking frightened. It is one of the few images of a naked and distinctly sexual woman in Sendak's art up to this time, which's combined with a man shooting a dead man, a gruesome illustration to one of the more gruesome Grimm stories. As Joyce Whalley and Tessa Chester put it in *A History of Children's Book Illumination*:

> *The densely cross-hatched backgrounds with their huge figures pressing against the frame give them a subtly intense claustrophic air cleverly balanced by the book's simple design and allowance of only one illustration per tale.* (235)

The figures in Maurice Sendak's Grimm book are massive: each one extends right to the edges of the frame. Other objects are squashed in around the main figure of each picture: for example, in *Spindle, Shuttle, and Needle* around the young women are plants, a window, a cupboard, a broom, a cat and a window. In the distance is the prince. The intense compression of the imagery appears claustrophic, but this very action of squeezing so much into the frame heightens the sense of unreality-in-the-midst-of-reality which Sendak searches for.

'The tales themselves are claustrophobic. They work on two levels: first, as stories; second, as the unravelling of deep psychological dramas', Maurice Sendak explained (AMS, 203). And he was most interested, of course, in the psychodrama level.

The illustration to *The Twelve Huntsmen* is dominated by one of Maurice Sendak's lions, in full Jacobean costume. Many of the Brothers Grimm pictures are like this: a crowded, intense foreground space with something happening in the middle distance. It's a visual configuration Sendak employed so successfully in *Outside Over There*, where the father's ship is seen on the sea. Sendak had shown, with his illustrations for *Zlateh the Goat and Other Stories*, his taste for highly compressed black-and-white images. In *The First Schlemiel*, from *Zlateh the Goat and Other Stories*, Sendak drew an old man as large as the picture frame, a technique he uses repeatedly. Beside the Sendakian motif of the open window is a large cockerel. On the floor is the Sendakian baby, looking unhappy. In *The Fool's Paradise* from *Zlateh the Goat and Other Stories*, the scene of a man in bed being tended by an old woman is rendered in a crowded mid-shot. Sendak fills the picture with details such as the bedside table with its candle, the bed covers, the patterned carpet, the old women's clothes and the bed's drapes. Sendak uses every inch of a picture, usually covering it with marks.

Maurice Sendak's stories of the Grimm Brothers romanticize the grinding poverty of the fairy stories just as the fairy tales themselves are romanticized versions of the abysmal conditions of the late 18th/ early 19th century proletariat and sub-proletariat. The appeal of fairy tales is partly that magic can manifest itself even in the dreariest of lives. In *Spindle, Shuttle, and Needle*, the common object of labour, the shuttle, becomes a magician. It weaves magic in the poor woman's house, helping her to draw the prince to her:

> *At once the shuttle leaped from her hand and out the door, and at the threshold it began to weave a carpet more beautiful than anything that you have seen: roses and lilies bloomed along the sides, and in the middle, on a field of gold, hares and rabbits leaped through green climbing vines from which stags and does raised up their heads; among the twigs sat colourful birds that did everything but sing. The shuttle scurried here and there; it was as if everything grew*

of itself. (JT, 58-61)

In the powerful *Hansel and Gretel* picture, the witch dominates the scene, taking up all of the frame vertically, and half the space horizontally. On the left hand half of the frame Maurice Sendak has managed to cram in Gretel kneeling before the witch, a large witch's cauldron, a shed in which Hansel is imprisoned, a Sendakian dog lying on the roof of the shed, and a background landscape of a tree and a full moon behind a wrack of clouds.

The effect has the vortiginous clarity of a dream, where every object is brought up close to the viewer. *Hansel and Gretel*, more than most fairy tales, enacts an intense œdipal crisis, which Maurice Sendak is conscious of evoking in his illustration. 'What is so sad in 'Hansel and Gretel'', says Sendak, 'is the father's passive acquiescence in letting his children die' (AMS, 201). It is indeed dismaying to a childlike mind that the father allows the second wife to dominate him and persuade him to leave his children alone in the forest (in Charles Perrault's version of *Tom Thumb*, both parents collude in losing their children in the forest). The father does get a second chance, because Hansel's resourcefulness saves him and his sister, when they follow the line of stones back home. It is at this point that the father, with his second chance to save his children, fails.

The witch then steps in, at the moment when the children are helpless and wide open to influence. It is the moment that parents fear, when their children are let loose in the big, dangerous world before they are ready to cope with it. The witch appears at first as the kindly parent, who has not just candy for her children, not just a cupboard full of candy, but a whole house made of candy and sweet things. The witch is a third stepmother, one of the clearest examples in fairy tales of the feared 'dark' aspect of the feminine. The witch is the Dark Mother, as the Goddess Kali is called in Indian religion. Gleefully, Kali decapitates her lovers and eats them: this is what the witch in *Hansel and Gretel* does, fattening up Hansel like an animal before the slaughter.

> *I think children read the internal meanings of everything. It's only adults who read the top layer most of the time* [remarked Sendak]. *I'm generalizing again, of course, but I'll bet my pictures don't surprise kids. They know what's in Grimm. They know that stepmother probably means mother, that the word step is there to avoid frightening older people. Children know there are mothers who abandon their children, emotionally if not literally. Sometimes they have to live with this fact. They don't lie to themselves.* (AMS, 205)

Like the son in Rembrandt van Rijn's *The Return of the Prodigal Son* (1669, Hermitage Museum), Maurice Sendak's Gretel kneels submissively before the towering figure of the witch. Significantly, Sendak said he was portraying 'the very second before she performs her fearless deed and becomes a *mensch*' (AMS, 201), that is, the moment when, like Rapunzel or Snow White, she grows up and becomes a self-responsible adult.

V

Sendak and Disney

MAURICE SENDAK IS always talking about *animation*, about pictures being 'dead' which are not 'animated', which are not 'quick' with life. Throughout his work, he speaks of a desire to 'animate' his stories, and in the trilogy, *Where the Wild Things, In the Night Kitchen* and *Outside Over There*, he comes close to a form of animation. *Wild Things*' pictures grow page by page, while *Night Kitchen*'s pictures are put beside each other, so that the eye flicks from one to the other. In Sendak's *œuvre*, music, dance, movement and animation are crucial: his idea of deadness in a children's book is a static picture. 'The spontaneous breaking into song and dance seems so natural and instinctive a part of childhood', he writes (C, 4).

Movement is crucial in Maurice Sendak's art. There is always movement in his pictures, always something going on. He is a restless, dynamic artist, a perfectionist, never satisfied, always questing after the next thing. He draws pictures to music, and many of his most fantastical illustrations are those drawn while particular pieces of music were playing: Johannes Brahms' *Violin Concerto*, Ludwig van Beethoven's *Quartet in F, Opus 135*, Franz Schubert's *Die Winterreise*, and Wolfgang Amadeus Mozart's *Quartet No. 19 in C* are some of the pieces of music that Sendak has improvized with, visually and graphically. He adores Giuseppe Verdi.

A key component of these musical dreams is the sense of transformation: babies changing into pigs, cats leaping out of smashed Humpty Dumpty eggs, and so on. Transformation is a crucial element in Maurice Sendak's art: characters are being transformed, either psychically or physically. The shape-shifting often occurs through the mouth – characters are eaten, then regurgitated as different characters. The dog in *Higglety Pigglety Pop!* eats then regurgitates a mop. In *Hector Protector* the monster swallows a ship. Food and eating form part of the background to *In the Night Kitchen*, in the city made of food and cooking utensils, and in the baking of the Mickey-cake. At the end of *Where the Wild Things Are*, the prize is... some hot food (a slice of cake, a glass of milk and a bowl of soup). Eating is very important for children, Sendak noted, and 'the Grimms' tales are full of things being eaten and then disgorged. It's an image that constantly appeals to me, and to most children too' (AMS, 239). (Some authors, such as J.K. Rowling and Roald Dahl, have fetishized food (candy especially) and eating to an extraordinary degree).

The physical transmutations are magical, and mirror or express inner, spiritual transformations. Drawings can do this so well, and cartoons can of course make these transformations occur seamlessly, showing each stage in the transformation, and the stages in between. But cartoons are of course still frames or cels shown at 24 frames (or pixels) per second, so the connections between 'static' drawings, on a page, and a cartoon on a cinema screen, are deep (even at its most digital and computerized, animation today still employs plenty of drawing by hand).

Always there is movement in these musical sketches. So it's no wonder that Maurice Sendak should love animated cartoons, and especially those of the Walt Disney Company. It's no surprise, either, that Sendak should be so disappointed with most of the cartoons dished up on Saturday mornings on children's television, because these modern cartoons are so 'dead', in Sendak's terminology. They are not 'alive', they are not 'quick'. There might be lots of movement in contemporary TV cartoons, but they are still lifeless. Besides, there is actually not much movement, literally, for movement in animation requires work. Due to economic constraints, many contemporary television cartoons are hardly 'animated' at all. Just an arm will move, or the eyes. It's astonishing how 'static' some animated cartoons are these days, when one looks closely at them. In *Where the Wild Things*, characters are often shown leaping about: Max is seen jumping, just about to land on the dog; Max's foot is stamping; he leaps with the Wild Things.

Maurice Sendak also laments the decline in standards in book manufacture, in the loss of traditional linotype faces, in the degeneration of the quality of paper. A book is a sacred object for Sendak, and every aspect of it must be considered thoughtfully: the paper (thickness, colour, surface, texture, etc), the size and the shape, the colours of the cover and binding, the typefaces used, and so on.

Maurice Sendak, like many other artists, remembers the very *smell* of certain books from childhood. Sendak aims to recapture some of the specialness of the books that one read as a child. Probably the greatest compliment one could pay Sendak would be to say that one had treasured his books as a child as he treasured certain books.

Music appears in other ways in Maurice Sendak's picture book art. Composers such as Wolfgang Amadeus Mozart are idols for Sendak, as they are for many artists.[1] Sendak included his own homage to Mozart in *Outside Over There*, where he depicts the composer sitting in a house in the background of one of the last pictures in the book. Sendak wrote:

> *In* Outside Over There *the little house makes its appearance as the summer cottage just outside Vienna where Mozart finished his* Magic Flute. (C, 198)

Maurice Sendak has cited Walt Disney many times, and especially Mickey Mouse. Mickey Mouse stories helped Sendak 'to get through the day' as a child, he said in 1982.[2]

You can see Mickey Mouse in his protagonists – explicitly in Mickey in *In the Night Kitchen*, but also in the feisty heroes of *Hector Protector, Where the Wild Things Are* and *Rosie.*

> *Best of all, our street pal was also a movie star* [remembered Sendak]. *In the darkened theater, the sudden flash of his brilliant, wild, joyful face – radiating great golden beams – filled me with an intoxicating, unalloyed pleasure.* (C, 108)

It is the early Mickey Mouse that Maurice Sendak likes, when the cartoon character was wilder than his later image. It is not Mickey's personality (the All-American Boy) Sendak enjoyed, however, but his graphic image (C, 108). In his childhood, the movies and radio were big influences. '*Fantasia* was *the* artistic experience of my childhood, and that was a mixed blessing', Sendak recalled (C, 175). Other movies, such as Laurel and Hardy, the 1933 *King Kong* and Busby Berkeley musicals were also a part of Sendak's childhood. No museums, though, no 'high art'. (Movies are a big deal for Sendak: he has also appeared in some: he's in *Angels In America*, playing a rabbi, and in *Amarcord*, Federico Fellini's 1973 childhood movie).

Easy to spot the soaring surrealism of *Fantasia* and other early Disney animated feature films in Maurice Sendak's work. His favourite Disney picture is *Pinocchio*:

> Pinocchio, *my favourite of the full-length Disneys, is a passionate film, shrewdly paced, overwhelmingly inventive. There are flaws (Cleo's fluttering eyelashes and the pallid, unctuous Blue Fairy, for example), but the emotional conviction of the drama far outweighs them.* (C, 182)

The Disney Studios censored the violence and 'negative' feelings of the original fairy tales, and substituted an illusion of 'happy ever after'. In the original fairy tales (by the Grimm Brothers, for instance), the utopian stance acknowledged social injustices and violence. Walt Disney himself edited that out, simplifying the fairy tales into an 'us and them', good against evil story. Walt Disney's *Snow White and the Seven Dwarfs* (1937), for instance, moved the emphasis away from a story of passion and retribution to the 'charm of little creatures'.[3] The two main protagonists of *Snow White* are clearly Snow White and the Queen/ Witch, and the drama comes from the tensions between them. Among the best moments of Disney's *Snow White* are undoubtedly those involving the witch and Snow White.[4]

But the Disney legacy remains as powerful as ever, particularly in those five feature animations of Disney's 'golden age': *Snow White and the Seven Dwarfs, Bambi, Dumbo, Pinocchio* and *Fantasia*. For many, those five films are the summit of cinematic animation, and remain high-water marks to this day. The power of those movies is undeniable, and in terms of artistry and emotional impact they have few equals (the movies of Hayao Miyazaki and Studio Ghibli are without question the equals of Disney Studios at its very height, and for some they surpass Disney). But for Disney's detractors, the Walt Disney Company means American imperialism on a grand scale, global popular culture which dumbs down its source material (fairy and folk tales) and colonizes other nations' cultures, Disneyfying them. Disney represents the zenith of late consumer capitalism and out-and-out materialism for anti-capitalists and leftwing/ liberal intellectuals. For them, Disney has wrecked the world of fairy tales, turning them into sentimental, saccharine slices of superficial entertainment, using fairy tales as a means of expanding a vast merchandizing and licensing empire, which feeds synergetically into theme parks, television, magazines, websites and stores. Thus, fairy tales become nothing more than eighty minute commercials for a range of toys and merchandizing.

Maurice Sendak remains on the artistic, dignified side of this debate, still clinging to modernist notions of the sacrality of the art object – the beautiful children's book. And still advocating the importance of meaning and value in a superficial, sound-bite, postmodern world. There's a pedagogic, moral aspect to Sendak's art which he won't let go of in a society of cel phones, computers, the internet, merchandizing, and global capitalism. For him, books still have a place, still *mean* something, still have a value, still have something to teach. They might be competing with computer games and teen magazines, celebrity culture and pop music (or new digital books), but they have something to offer.

Maybe the Western world is sliding towards a pre-dominantly 'visual culture', a world of TV news and MTV, leaving the written word behind, but Maurice Sendak does have one powerful weapon: fabulous images. And no one else produces imagery quite like Sendak's (an important distinction in a world of thousands and millions of images). Further, words have endured, despite the expansion of the digital realm into all areas of Western life. Without words, images float around, increasingly directionless and affectless, swiftly replaced by more images.

VI

✪

Where the Wild Things Are

MAURICE SENDAK'S FIRST big success was *Where the Wild Things Are* (1963). It was the book which marked a turning-point in his career as an illustrator. In a way, Sendak will always be remembered as the author of *Where the Wild Things Are*, if for nothing else (it has sold 19 million copies, up to 2011). It is the first in a trilogy of books about the primal experiences of being a child, about dealing with 'anger, boredom, fear, frustration, jealousy', as Sendak put it (AMS, 227).

Maurice Sendak remarked of *Where the Wild Things Are*:

> *Max is my bravest and therefore my dearest creation. Like all children, he believes in a flexible world of fantasy and reality, a world where a child can skip from one to the other and back again in the sure belief that both really exist. Another quality that makes him especially lovable to me is the directness of his approach. Max doesn't shilly-shally about.* (C, 152)

Where the Wild Things Are grew out of a dream, or a fantasy. It is a dream, though, based in fantasy, and Maurice Sendak begins his most famous book with some naturalistic scenes and settings: Max building a 'camp' in his home, and chasing the dog down the stairs with a fork. A sketch for the picture where Max's building a tent shows a scene of pandemonium: a lamp is set on a cardboard box; his mom's hat hangs from a wire hanger, a banana hangs from a bit of string, a boot is stuck in a hanging pot. Max is shown holding onto the rope, kicking his legs and hollering, a pose later used when he reaches the Land of the Wild Things. On a bed sheet, Max has drawn a monster's face.

Where the Wild Things Are begins with some playacting – Max is wearing his wolf-suit.[1] He is pretending to be a 'wild thing', and ends up being too much of a wild thing, for his mother calls him a wild thing and sends him to bed. One expects to see the irate mother, but Maurice Sendak concentrates on Max. One would expect to see just how angry his mother is, but it is Max's response that Sendak regards as important. Max's mischief seems to be just mischief, nothing very bad. But Max gets sent to bed, which's quite a serious telling-off, and Max is shown looking forlorn alone in his room. Max's mischief (his 'joyous anarchy'),[2] links up with his handling of the Wild Things. Max can be fierce – not only in his mischief, but also in his dealings with the Wild Things. Any worries which might have arisen from the text that Max might not be able to handle the Wild Things are dispelled not only when we see Max's behaviour in the Land of the Wild Things, but also when we see his fierce mischief-making.

The look of the 1963 book is a generalized mid-20th century: the furnishings, costumes and props suggest a world that could be a Moscow town house or a Sydney suburb as well as somewhere in Middle America. Maurice Sendak deliberately keeps out modern technology, such as televisions, radios, and myriad household appliances (which often date badly). Max might be playing in the middle of the 19th century, or the Depression, as well as the early Sixties, when *Where the Wild Things Are* was published.

Maurice Sendak's text plays with the reader's conventional expectations. For example, the first page says 'The night Max wore his wolf suit and made mischief of one kind', then leaves a gap before the completion of the sentence on the next page: 'and another'. Sendak's book creates a tension between anticipation and fulfilment, for, to take in the first page the reader has to read not only the text but also the picture. The balance between the text and picture on the first page is not even: the unfinished sentence bids the reader to turn over, but the picture demands that the reader linger. The sequence of these two pages with the incomplete sentence suggests a *series* of mischiefs, of 'one kind... and another... and another... and another'. There might be a chase shown, for instance, with Max trying to escape his angry mother.

The power of children to create fantastical worlds is very apparent in *Where the Wild Things Are.* Significantly, at first Max does not 'travel' to the Land of the Wild Things. It comes to him, or rather, he creates it. He stands in his bedroom, calmly tapping his foot while the Wild Things World materializes behind him. Max is quite confident about his imaginative powers. As he taps his foot, eyes closed, he knows the world of the Wild Things is taking shape behind him (he doesn't need to look).

The transformation of Max's bedroom into the Land of the Wild Things shows how powerful children's imaginations can be. It shows that Max's game making a camp or chasing the dog is *real.* Real and not real, real and *more real.* Only when he's created his own universe does Max voyage across it in his own 'private boat'.

In the 1955 *Where the Wild Horses Are,* the prototype story for *Where the Wild Things Are*, the child follows some signs to the Wild Horses place. In *Where the Wild Things Are*, however, Max creates the Wild Things world himself. Max shows himself to be more powerful than the Wild Things, who are not that scary after all; the *text alone* might suggest that the monsters are frightening and Max is the one who is scared; the *pictures* show who finally attains mastery. The pictures are not that scary, but on its own, the text is: the reader could imagine far more horrific monsters than the ones Maurice Sendak depicts. For example, when Max meets the group of Wild Things, in the first picture that runs right across two pages, he leans on the side of his boat, one hand on his hip, frowning, as if he's a parent mightily displeased with the Wild Things' childish behaviour. In the picture where Max returns over the ocean, he looks quite nonchalant, unimpressed by being in the midst of an adventure story and fairy tale.

Maurice Sendak's protagonists share common characteristics. For instance, there are different versions of Max (Rosie, Martin, Kenny), who, says Sendak, 'all have the same need to master the uncontrollable and frightening aspects of their lives, and they all turn to fantasy to accomplish this.' (C, 152)

An early draft of the words for *Where the Wild Things Are* read:

> *Once a boy asked where the wild horses are. Nobody could tell him. So he asked himself where the wild horses are. And he answered, they must be this way. Luckily the way led through his own room. He found signs pointing in the right direction.* (AMS, 88)

The early draft for *Where the Wild Things Are*, composed in April 1963, was over-written ('The rug on his floor was the grassy path into the forest'). The dummy for *Where the Wild Things Are* still contained some unnecessary sections of the story, as when the narrator says that 'Max didn't care because the Wild Things never... let him eat from grown-up plates, or showed him how to call long distance' (AMS, 96).

Thankfully, Maurice Sendak severely pruned the story down to 348 words. He realized that his pictures could do a lot of the talking and describing. In the original story of *Where the Wild Things Are*, the monster's mother appears, changing into a wolf. So Sendak's story would have featured those startling images of transformation which Sendak drew as he listened to Wolfgang Amadeus Mozart. Sendak dropped the idea of shape-changing, although it is hinted at in Max's wolf suit. Indeed, Max appears more than half-wolf in the early sketches: there are no buttons shown on his front, so the only obvious visual sign that Max's human is the face and the costume's hood (and standing upright); the rest of him is wolf.

Maurice Sendak changed the horses to 'things' or monsters for a practical reason: he couldn't really draw horses. Interestingly, Sendak's based his 'wild things' on relatives who came round every Sunday when he was a child (AMS, 88). *King Kong* influenced the depiction of the Wild Things too, and a friend of Sendak's pointed out that one of the pictures in *Where the Wild Things Are* is a dead ringer for a shot in *King Kong* (the 1933 monster movie, which's probably haunted many impressionable imaginations, would crop up in the follow-up to *Where the Wild Things Are*, *In the Night Kitchen*).

✪

The pictures in *Where the Wild Things Are* grow and contract. As the fantasy increases, so the pictures expand in size. As the pictures grow, the words diminish, relative to the pictures. Just before and after the wild rumpus there is a balance between words and pictures on each page. The three central double-page spreads are triumphant examples of book illustration (not just *children's* book illustration).

The book has its climax in the middle, not, as is usual, at the end. Here, the pictures expand so much they bleed off the page, leaving no room for words. The totality of the central pictures means they are no longer framed; there is no longer an extra distance between the reader and the pictures. The pictures are seen as from 'within', as a total experience. The pictures in the book expand, first on one page, then they move across the left-hand page.[3] The white space around the text becomes broken into as the tree and edges of the pictures spread across the left-hand pages. Here something forbidden and miraculous breaks the frame around the pictures.[4] We see the Wild Things hanging on trees like monkeys, copying Max and kicking their legs, grimacing, having a great time. We see the Wild Things howling at the moon, dancing in an ancient ritual. This scene replays the earlier one from *The Moon Jumpers*. It has a primitive, ritual aspect which Maurice Sendak conjures up with apparent ease. Yet the pictures are dark and mysterious and strangely still.

My favourite picture from these large pictures is where the Wild Things are marching in a procession, with Max crowned as King of the Wild Things, riding on one of beast's backs. He holds his sceptre aloft, his eyes closed in that mood of cool confidence which we saw when Max created the Land of the Wild Things in his bedroom. Technically, it might have been more difficult for the artist to draw the Wild Things being frightened of Max when he tames them by staring into their eyes, but it is the procession illustration that marks the highpoint of *Where the Wild Things Are*. There is no sky, and the colours are dark with much crosshatching in the shadowy leaf background.[5]

This is one of Maurice Sendak's finest illustrations, and the image rightly appears on publicity material for *Where the Wild Things Are* and Sendak's books. It is also on the cover of *The Art of Maurice Sendak*. This picture is the apotheosis of *Where the Wild Things Are*: it is Max's crowning moment, and after this the pictures contract as Max calls a halt to the rumpus. After the rumpus, the pictures begin to diminish until, on the last page, there is no picture and just four words.[6]

One odd example of continuity in *Where the Wild Things Are* is the appearances of the monsters. Basically, they swap around. On one page we see the one with the stripy sweater and rounded face, on another page the one with long orange hair and bird-like feet. On another page, the dark Wild Thing with bull's horns. This can be confusing for children, who sometimes expect a logical continuity.

The pictures are marked by a surprising amount of green and blue, sombre colours for illustrating noise and action. Many of the pictures, such as the ones depicting the transformation of Max's bedroom into the forest, are dark and shadowy. Some of the picture have a blue cast in them, as if they've been filmed in 'day for night'. At the end of the story, of course, Max's bedroom warms up, with pink and yellows. The scale of the objects in the final picture is larger, too, making the atmosphere cosier, so that Max is not so isolated in a space of his own, as he is in the first picture. Odd too that the cover 'gives away' one of the secrets of the book, by showing a sleeping monster.

The cover of *Where the Wild Things Are* offers some ambiguities for the young reader. What, for example, is the 'Wild Thing' of the title? Is it the sleeping monster seen on the cover? It looks like a wild beast, but it is shown sleeping. The cover picture's atmosphere is of calm and quiet. On the title page, another picture shows some more 'Wild Things', and also, a thing dressed up as a 'Wild Thing', a boy in his wolf-suit. Maybe this is also meant to be one of the 'Wild Things' of the title. Later it becomes apparent that the boy is indeed one of the 'Wild Things' (his mother calls him 'WILD THING', and Max becomes known as 'the wildest thing of all').

✪

Where the Wild Things Are grows out of the despair that comes from (a child) being abandoned. Being sent to his bedroom alone for the evening is potentially a traumatic time for Max. And even after the wild rumpus, when Max might be expected to be flushed with joy, he sits, hand on chin, wistful, in his tent, apart from the sleeping Wild Things, whom he has sent to bed. The book is founded on the experience of being abandoned, as Bruno Bettelheim noted:

> *The basic anxiety of the child is desertion. To be sent to bed alone is one desertion, and without food is the second desertion. The combination is the worst desertion that can threaten a child.*[7]

The key message of *Where the Wild Things Are* is the child's imaginative ability to turn a potentially horrible situation into a more positive one. *Where the Wild Things Are* is about the triumph of fantasy and imagination over the horrific aspects of life.

> *Through fantasy, Max, the hero of my book* [remarked Sendak], *discharges his anger against his mother, and returns to the real world sleepy, hungry, and at peace with himself.* ("Caldecott Medal Acceptance", 151)

For Maurice Sendak, *Where the Wild Things Are* was a story of a journey of catharsis, a way through fantasy to calm. In the book, Sendak said, his hero learns how to make sense of the confusing, difficult world. He learns how to overcome fear and anxiety through fantasy and imagination. As Sendak says, 'it is through fantasy that children achieve catharsis. It is the best means they have for taming Wild Things.' (C, 151) And again, Sendak stated:

> *Max, too, is having fun, and not by playing hide-and-seek with Sigmund Freud. He is delighted at having conjured up his horrific beasts, and their willingness to be ordered about by an aggressive miniature king is, for Max, his wildest dream come true. My experience suggests that the adults who are troubled by the suggestions of his fantasy forget that my hero is having the time of his life and that he controls the situation with breezy aplomb.* (C, 152-3)

The strong bonds of love between Max and his mother are displayed in their fierce interchange, where the Sendakian motif of eating becomes the metaphor for love: 'I'LL EAT YOU UP' cries Max. This at first seems to be a threat of violence. Only later does it become apparent that the expression of eating is linked to the mother-child bond of love, when the Wild Things, desperate to keep Max with them, cry 'We'll eat you up, we love you so'. The erotic and emotional aspects of eating become clear (this was seen in Maurice Sendak's musical improvizational drawings of the 1950).

Maurice Sendak's text evokes the fierce emotions between parents and children, emotions which go right back to the erotic, semiotic, pre-œdipal and pre-symbolic mother-child dyad (*pace* Julia Kristeva, via Sigmund Freud and Jacques Lacan). So deep and so thorough are the emotions flowing between parents and children they cannot help but produce moments of agony, fear, confusion, and intense desire. The eating metaphor ('I'LL EAT YOU UP') expresses this in suitably childish and childlike language, a poetry of oral psychology which is not confined at all to childhood, but runs deeply through people throughout their lives.

The frustration that Max feels, then, is deep and agonizing. He has had his wildness curtailed: there must be somewhere else for it to go, so powerful is it. Very quickly, it flows outward towards the creation of the Land of the Wild Things. Instead of being eaten by his mother, which is an expression of her potentially suffocating love (the œdipal agony of having to escape the parent, the simultaneously loved and loathed parent), Max goes on the rampage, and 'eats' up the Wild Things by taming them. Their way of trying to keep him there is by threatening to eat him up. The Wild Things are clearly parental equivalents, something like parents, to be feared and desired. The continuity between the mother and the Wild Things is emphasized by the original version, in which the monsters' mother appears, changing into a wolf.

In *Where the Wild Thing Are* a common thread running through the story is wildness, as a metaphor or equivalent for the bonds of love between people, especially children and parents. Wildness is what happens when love is not focussed: instead of eating and being eaten slowly, tenderly, in a mutual embrace, parental-child love becomes an aggressive shout of 'I'LL EAT YOU UP'; that is, I'll destroy you. Poetic links are made between wolves-wildness-love-mothers-Wild Things-eating-food-parental relationships.

In *Where the Wild Thing Are* each of three main characters – Max, his mother and the Wild Things – veers between the extremes of love and wildness. The Wild Things are first aggressive and 'terrible', then they are calmed; when Max threatens to leave, they become tender, but express their love in a suitably monsterish fashion ('We'll eat you up, we love you so'). This is a dramatic turnaround of affairs in the portrayal of the Wild Things, and it is Maurice Sendak's triumph that he can make them appear loving as well as still Wild Thingish and 'terrible'.

The mother expresses both love and wildness for Max. She sends him to bed in anger when his wildness becomes too much, but halfway through the story her love for Max pervades the boy, as he wishes for love and to be where there were good things to eat. Again, the eating metaphor expresses child-parent love. When the food does appear, and is still hot, this is 'unspeakable and unseeable motherlove'.[8] Max, meanwhile, travels from states of wildness and mischief, through rejection and solitude, to dream and imagination, to fear (of the Wild Things), to triumph (as he controls them), to, importantly, a yearning for motherly love, which's finally rewarded. It is significant that what turns the story about, what urges Max back to his home, is not any actions of the Wild Things, but Max's remembrance of being loved.

JULIA KRISTEVA ON MOTHERS, ARTISTS AND EARLY PSYCHOSEXUAL GROWTH

THE WRITINGS OF Julia Kristeva, the French philosopher, are particularly illuminating in discussing the realm of the mother and the role of the artist or poet in relation to Maurice Sendak's art. Max, like some of Sendak's other characters, embodies some of the tensions that Julia Kristeva has explored in her work on the *chora* or semiotic realm, the mother, and how early psychosexual growth relates to the artist. In the Kristevan system, the (male) child must split up his mother in order to take up his masculine gender: she is split into the abject and the sublime.[9] Abjecting the mother enables the child to separate himself from the mother. To counter the mother becoming a phobic object, if she is only abjected, the phobic substitutes a sign for the absent object (ib., 45). Abjection thus operates in an in-between zone, as Kristeva calls it, 'of phobia, obsessions, and perversion' (ib.). A loving 'imaginary' father is necessary for this journey through the stages of Kristevan abjection (think of the Wild Things): the imaginary constructs encourage the separation from the mother. Only when the child identifies with the space opened up by the archaic or imaginary father, the paternal space, 'the father of individual pre-history',[10] can narcissism occur.

All this leads to one of Julia Kristeva's most provocative ideas, that of the *chora* and the semiotic modality, which was so eloquently explored in *Révolution du langue poétique*, one of Kristeva's key theoretical texts. For Kristeva, the *chora* is an archaic, pre-œdipal space, linked to the semiotic modality, a realm of ambiguity, uncertainty, undetermined articulation. It occurs in a phase of mother-child *jouissance* and polymorphous perversity, a time of rhythmic, heterogeneous impulses before the child enters the symbolic realm. The *chora* is the place where the subject is generated and negated. The sounds associated with the semiotic realm include laughter and word-games, the voice seen as rhythm and tone, and the body in its motion and rhythm. The word *chora* means receptacle in Greek, Kristeva explained.

From the *chora* and semiotic flows poetry (or art). This is where things get very interesting. Artistic creation becomes a struggle involving signification, transgression, the semiotic and the symbolic. The semiotic is revolutionary because of the way in which the psychological subject has been made up since the Enlightenment: the semiotic can be a means of transgressing the (masculine) symbolic.[11] As Julia Kristeva comments (again, this throws light on the parent-child tension at work in *Where the Wild Things Are*):

> *And so, according to psychoanalysis, poets as individuals fall under the category of fetishism; the very practice of art necessitates reinvesting the maternal* chora *so that it transgresses the symbolic order... the poetic function therefore converges with fetishism; it is not, however, identical to it. What distinguishes the poetic function from the fetishist mechanism is that it maintains a* signification *(*Bedeutung*). All its paths into, indeed valorizations of, pre-symbolic semiotic stases not only require the ensured maintenance of this signification but also serve signification, even when they dislocate it. No text, no matter how 'musicalized', is devoid of meaning or signification; on the contrary,*

musicalization pluralizes meanings. We may say therefore that the text is not a fetish. (1986, 115-6)

It is no good remaining in the semiotic modality however, much as one might like to (much as Max would like to remain in the Land of the Wild Things): one would not have a position or social signification from which to speak. No, one must enter the symbolic realm. If one does not enter the symbolic realm, psychosis may result.

Julia Kristeva's marvellous evocation of the semiotic realm or *chora* offers alternative ways of looking at Maurice Sendak's *Where the Wild Things Are*: the Wild Things can be seen as father figures, in the Freudian manner, with the land of adventure that Max travels to being a stand-in for the symbolic or œdipal realm. Or his encounter with the Wild Things might be seen as an entry into a semiotic realm, a mother world, and Max has to return to the symbolic realm, the Law of the Father. Maybe if he stayed in the Land of the Wild Things he would become truly wild, and lose his humanity. Maybe the story is about the need for *both* realms – home and wilderness, domesticity and adventure. Maybe it's about the need for a *balance* between the two.

VI

In the Night Kitchen

IN THE NIGHT KITCHEN (1970) is Maurice Sendak's homage to Americana, to the glitz and surreal nature of the street furniture, the oddness of the American signs, billboards and advertizing, the strangeness of a city at night. The city is of course New York City, the place that Sendak dreamt about in his childhood, the great American metropolis. '*In the Night Kitchen* is a kind of homage to New York City, the city I loved so much and still love' (C, 175). (Later, Sendak moved to rural Connecticut). Gotham was a magical place for the young Maurice Sendak: trips there were something like magical journeys.

> Night Kitchen *and, to a lesser degree,* Wild Things *reflect a popular American art both crass and oddly surrealistic, an art that encompasses the Empire State Building, syncopated Disney cartoons, and aluminium-clad comic-book heroes, an Art Moderne that was most sensuously catalogued in the movies.* (C, 167)

In the Night Kitchen looks to the Busby Berkeley musicals of the 1930s, and Mickey Mouse; *Where the Wild Things Are* to monster movies (in particular *King Kong*); *Higglety Pigglety Pop!* looks to 19th century illustration (C, 167). As Maurice Sendak writes in his "Hans Christian Andersen Medal Acceptance" speech, the 'pleasurably dreaded movie monsters, the graphically vivid, absurdly endearing figures of Mickey Mouse and Charlie Chaplin were the most direct influence on me as a young artist'. (C, 170)

The heart of *In the Night Kitchen* grows from a childhood desire to escape into fantasy, embodied in the yearning to join in having fun at night. Maurice Sendak recalls seeing an ad in his childhood for Sunshine Bakers which said 'We Bake While You Sleep!' For Sendak, this was cruel, because he wanted to join them: 'all I wanted to do was stay up and watch'.[1] Mickey's task, then, the problem he has to solve, is how to stay up all night (C, 208).

As with many of Maurice Sendak's other books, *In the Night Kitchen* is about subverting the moral and social order of parents. Like *Where the Wild Things Are, In the Night Kitchen*'s wild goings-on occur at night. While *Where the Wild Things Are* moves in a cycle from evening through night to morning, most of *In the Night Kitchen* occurs at night. It is a night of madness. The book is full of images of being helpless, of falling – Mickey falls out of his bed, he falls into bread dough, he falls into milk, he flies up in a plane, he is nearly burned alive in an oven. *In the Night Kitchen* is very much about the wildness of what can happen at night. It is about reverting to a primitive order of life, where physical acts predominate over reason and logic.[2]

> *I have written a new picture-book text* [wrote Sendak], *and I'm mad for it – and* it's *mad... It comes from the direct middle of me, and it hurt like hell extracting it. Yes, indeed, very birth-delivery type pains, and it's about as regressed as I imagine I can go. Simply, it's divine.*[3]

It is very sexual, too, with its images of Mickey being smothered by cake dough, falling into milk, and cavorting nude (one critic – Perry Nodelman in *Words About Pictures: The Narrative Art of Children's Picture Books* – saw Mickey's sensual antics as having 'clearly masturbatory connotations – if one wants to think of it in those terms' [1988, 109]). *In the Night Kitchen* is Sendak's 'oddest, most revealing attempt to uncover his own libido', according to some critics (for Joyce Whalley and Tessa Chester put it in *A History of Children's*

Book Illumination, 209). Some censorious detractors drew pants on Mickey in books housed in libraries.

Maurice Sendak reacted strongly when people criticized the nudity of *In the Night Kitchen*. He made an interesting point by comparing nudity in 'popular' art such as *In the Night Kitchen* with high art such as Roman and Greek statues:

> *They told me you can't have a penis in a book for children; it frightens them. Yet parents take their children to museums where they see Roman statues with their dicks broken off. You'd think that would frighten them more.* (AMS, 189)

The comparison with high art automatically exalts Maurice Sendak's efforts. One of Sendak's specialities is naked children. The boy David in *Fly By Night* is nude; the goblins in *Outside Over There* are nude; the Princess in *The Light Princess* is naked; Mr Rabbit is also nude in *Mr Rabbit and the Lovely Present*. The sleeping male nude is also favoured by Sendak (in *Fly By Night* and *Mr Rabbit and the Lovely Present*). And in works of the 1980s up to the present, nudity – and sexuality – is a recurring ingredient.

In *Outside Over There*, though, as with *In the Night Kitchen*, nudity is not made an issue of by the author. For Mickey, it's a natural state, parallelling nudity as a return to innocence. With the group of goblins as naked babies, only one of them is posed so the genitals can be seen. The nudity of the babies is no more unusual than nude cherubs in Italian Renaissance altarpieces (although in contemporary times linking children with nudity in art is fraught with problems).

✪

Mickey in *In the Night Kitchen* is all over the place. On the very first page he is somersaulting out of bed. He falls into dough, then is seen pounding it into the shape of a plane. Mickey is all action, all movement. He won't keep still. Very quickly, after being disturbed by the noise ('QUIET DOWN THERE!'), Mickey takes matters into his own hands. He does not take any nonsense from anyone, and is shown in some very proud, cocky poses, culminating when, like a cockerel, he shouts 'COCK-A-DOODLE-DOO!' Throughout *In the Night Kitchen* Mickey is 'well on his way'. He makes bold, assertive statements, such as

QUIET DOWN THERE!
I'm not the milk, and the milk's not me, I'm Mickey!
God bless milk, and God bless me
COCK-A-DOODLE-DOO!

Mickey is without question Maurice Sendak's most positive, life-affirming protagonist. The wistful melancholy of characters such as Kenny does not cling to him. Indeed, Mickey very distinctly throws off the trappings of culture and society when he falls out of his clothes. His nudity asserts his primal purity. 'I'm Mickey!'

The flight in a plane of his own making re-enacts the essential dream moment, which is flying. Mickey's flight is the magical flight of the archaic shaman, the befeathered dreamer who can magically travel to other worlds. Many of Maurice Sendak's protagonists exhibit this shamanic ability to fly. Ida flies when she puts on her mother's yellow coat (the garment, and pulling it on, recalls shamanic shape-changing, like Max's wolf-suit). The naked boy in *Fly By Night* is like a more grown-up Mickey the pilot. He is shown flying even as he's dreaming. The characters in *Sarah's Room* and *I Want To Paint My Bathroom Blue* also fly. Flying is one of the recurring motifs of dreaming and both flying and dreaming (and flying within dreams) have an erotic component.

Mickey's dive into the giant milk bottle called the Milky Way has of course a mythological precedent. It recalls the ancient phrase 'a kid, I fell into milk'. It occurs in the Welsh *Mabinogion*, where the child Gwion tastes the magical cauldron of the terrifying Goddess and witch Cerridwen and is transformed into the poet-genius Taleissin. In Greek mythology, the Milky Way or galaxy was formed when the Goddess Rhea's milk gushed into the sky after the birth of the child Zeus.[4]

Mickey's emergence from the milk clearly has a religious or symbolic dimension. There is an alchemical element, too, with the giant milk bottle standing in for the alchemical vessel. Alchemical processes, especially of heating in the oven and cooling down in the milk, are central to the story. The triumph of the transformation is made clear by Mickey's call of 'COCK-A-DOODLE-DOO!'.

✪

The graphic qualities of *In the Night Kitchen* make it Maurice Sendak's boldest effort. It is not a book of subtleties, though they are there if one wishes to dig them out. The many cultural references are embedded in the pictures if one fancies searching for them. The pictures, though, are thoroughly joyous in their in-your-face starkness. One only has to look back to early colour books, such as *The Moon Jumpers*, to see how far Sendak had developed his style by the time of *In the Night Kitchen.* The colours are flat, but at the same time, there are some subtle hues to be found – in the central double-page spread, for instance, where lilacs sit next to pale blues and greens. On the left are soft crimsons next to beiges, prussian blues and lemon yellows, while the floor of this cosmic kitchen is grey and lilac. Despite the boldness of the imagery – the thick black lines around each object, the huge scale of the Laurel & Hardy cooks, the high energy of the narrative – many of the colours are in fact soft pastels.

The city is ingeniously constructed out of egg whisks, cork-screws, nutcrackers, beaters, sieves, condiments (a cake icer does for the Chrysler Building), and a dazzling variety of mass-produced food packaging. The abundance of the human-made world vies with that of nature in Maurice Sendak's portrayal of the city as a place of excess, of New York as the archetypal modern megalopolis. The amount of typographic data alone is enormous: there are signs of 'Kneitel's Fandango', 'Woody's Salt', 'Pure Cream', 'Phoenix Baking Soda', 'Hosmer's Free Running Sugar', 'Good, Great! Shortening', 'Clown Cleanser', '10¢', 'Philip's Best Tomatoes',

'Chase-O, Washes and Blues at One Time', 'Patented June 10th 1928, Registered Cocoanuts', 'Safe Yeast (Up with the Moon)', 'Ta-Ka-Kake', 'Baby Syrup', 'Infant Food, Price 42¢', 'Rolled White Oats', '150 Meals For $1.00', 'Schickel' and 'Mama's Cream of Tartar'. (But that's very much a part of the contemporary American cityscape – the amount of commercial signage on display all over the U.S.A. is staggering).

Maurice Sendak integrates his text with the images in a vigorous way. As with comicbooks, the text is very much regarded as a part of the overall design. Sometimes the words are so large they take up an entire frame on their own, as when Mickey shouts 'QUIET DOWN THERE', or when he shouts his victory call 'COCK-A-DOODLE DOO!' Here the physical scale of the words corresponds to the loudness of Mickey's enunciations.

In *Outside Over There* Maurice Sendak went further into exploring the physicality of the visual appearance of words, having them mounted on floating labels or boards in the midst of the action. These mounted-label pieces of text are theatrical, emphasizing the sense of theatrical illusion of the book form, with its inter-connected texts and illustrations. Also, they all relate to Ida's parents – Ida's father's song, for example – which gives them an added psychological dimension.

The cover of *In the Night Kitchen* shows one of the ecstatic moments in the story, Mickey's flight upward in the plane. There is a sky of stars and a full moon, and the cityscape of food packaging and utensils. The cover depicts Mickey in the midst of the Night Kitchen. The back cover has an image which's repeated three times: Mickey is shown clad in bread dough holding an enormous bottle of milk. This image appears on the half-title page, and on the final page, each time with a different background. The title page replays the cover, but without the New York City background. Maurice Sendak was in a happy typographic mood when he made the title page – he put blue stars on top of each letter 'i' in the title (which they didn't need, being capital letters). The dedication page ('for Sadie and Philip') also shows Mickey in his cake plane.

As always a full moon in Maurice Sendak's work presides over the nighttime revelry. Taken together, the symbolism is thoroughly redolent of female energy and maternal feelings. The milk, the cooking, the oven (as womb), the cosmic Night Kitchen with its baby food and the full moon make this maternal symbolism explicit. As Sendak notes, *In the Night Kitchen* marks an ultimate regression, to a primal state of existence. Falling into the cosmic milk is obviously a motif of spiritual rebirth. The trope of religious rebirth is also underlined by the nudity of Mickey. He changes from being clogged up with bread dough to being triumphantly naked. Milk is one of the sexual fluids of femininity and the maternal realm, and though all the protagonists we see in *In the Night Kitchen* are male, the spiritual foundation or source of power of Mickey's heroic, alchemical transformation is feminine and maternal. Again, as with *Where the Wild Things Are*, the child-mother relation is the source of love and nurturance. Again, food is the image of maternal nourishment – the milk and cake in *Night Kitchen*, the glass of milk and food in *Wild Things*. Though she is not seen, the mother is crucial to both *In the Night Kitchen* and *Where the Wild Things Are*; significantly, Sendak chose to make the mother visually central in two of his next major books, *Outside Over There* and *Dear Mili*.

VII

Outside Over There

OUTSIDE OVER THERE (1981) is the third book in the *Where the Wild Things Are* trilogy. It is the most sophisticated of the three, visually, and the most poignant and yearning of the trilogy.[1] '*Outside Over There* is the most personal of my books,' remarked Maurice Sendak, 'and my favourite.' (C, 208) The book operates on three levels (AMS, 227), Sendak explained, while *In the Night Kitchen* works on two (Mickey's story plus the 1930s/ New York imagery), and *Where the Wilds Things Are* on one level (simply, Max's story).

Outside Over There is also about fear – the fear of being stolen away by goblins, about the fear of loss, of losing one's child, one's father, and mother. Maurice Sendak identified himself with the child who is stolen by goblins in the book. The older sister he identifies as his own older sister. (Sendak had treated a similar theme in his illustration for the Grimms' *The Goblins*, where a baby is stolen by goblins, an image Sendak regarded as 'perhaps the single most successful drawing' in *The Juniper Tree* [AMS, 203]).

Outside Over There, like *Dear Mili,* is about the agony of losing the mother-world, the comfort and security of being inside the mother's house, which is the mother's body. Like *Where the Wild Things Are*, *Outside Over There* is about the anxiety of being a child, of having an ambiguous relationship with one's parents. It is about œdipal conflict. Significantly, throughout the book the father is never seen: the Law of the Father is present as a ship on a raging sea, and as a letter at the end which bids Ida to look after her baby brother and her mother. 'Sailor Papa' is shown as a worker, someone who goes out into the untamed world (the stormy seas) to work for his family. He is the husband and father as brave hunter-gatherer. He is not a homely farmer or shepherd tending his sheep (as other men are shown in *Outside Over There*), but is a courageous sailor who weathers storms. Sailor Papa has magic too – he has a sea chant which functions as a magical song in the traditional fairy tale manner (like *Mirror, mirror on the wall* in *Snow White*).

Maurice Sendak also mentions in connection with *Outside Over There* the following: seeing in his childhood a picture of a girl in a yellow coat; the eggshells are found in the Grimms' *Goblins* story; in the early 1930s, there was Eddie Cantor dressed as a baby; the Dionne quintuplets (echoed in the five goblins); Baby Snooks; and, importantly for Sendak, the Lindbergh case, when a baby was snatched. These cases always seem to strike a chord with the general public, or at least with the popular media. It's like the opposite of Christmas: instead of a baby being brought into the world, one is taken away. When he was young, Sendak identified with the snatched baby. This anxiety resurfaced in *Outside Over There*, so that the book became 'my exorcism of the Lindbergh case', as Sendak put it (C, 210). Like most (all?) children's books, Sendak's *Outside Over There* has a happy ending: like Max and Mickey, Ida wins through. She is brave, and succeeds in rescuing her sister.

Outside Over There involves a strong relationship between the main characters: where Max's pivotal relationship is with his mother, and Mickey's is with the parental stand-ins, the three cooks, Ida's main relationship is not with her mother, but with her sister. Ida reacts ambiguously to her sister and mother. First, she flies into a rage, when she realizes the baby has been stolen. Her anger is also directed at her mother for leaving the baby unattended. She resents but also loves the baby, and she 'does the right thing'.

Stylistically, *Outside Over There* is set in the latter part of the 18th century, the era of Wolfgang Amadeus Mozart (1756-91). Not only is there a *hommage* to Mozart, there are scenes taken from *The Magic Flute* (1791). It's all about Mozart. Maurice Sendak also used Philipp Otto Runge's (1777-1810) paintings, and Caspar David Friedrich (1774-1840).[2] The baby in *Outside Over There* is based, like most of the babies in Sendak's art, on the artist himself. Babies appear in much of his output – the giant baby in *The Juniper Tree*, the Bee-Man who becomes a baby in *The Bee-Man of Orn*, and the baby in *Higglety Pigglety Pop!*. In *Higglety Pigglety Pop!* the baby gets into all sorts of predicaments, including fending off a gigantic lion, the Downstairs Lion. The baby wears a floppy bonnet and nightgown, like Sendak's other babies. It is *Outside Over There*, however, that foregrounds babies most eloquently and emotively. The baby here is snatched, and the 1981 book is based on the trauma of the child being lost then recovered. While Max and Mickey rebirth themselves through fantasy, Ida has to rebirth (or save the life of) another human being.

The written text for *Outside Over There* is, like *Where the Wild Things Are* and *In the Night Kitchen*, short (359 words). Though short, the text to *Outside Over There* is poetic, and uses some of Maurice Sendak's idiosyncratic turns of phrase. Sendak employs deliberately old-fashioned phrases, so his texts seem not American but more like 19th century British works. Sendak uses compressions of phrases, because he's always trying to keep his text as short as possible, but also to retain the vividness. Thus, the goblins say 'we're dancing sick', instead of, in the more logical manner, 'we're sick and tired of dancing'. Instead of shortening this to 'we're sick of dancing', Sendak writes 'we're dancing sick'. This sort of compression occurs all the time in Sendak's books. The text for *Outside Over There* apparently went through a hundred drafts.

The pictures for *Outside Over There* are lush, as with 1988's *Dear Mili*. Like so many Renaissance artists, Maurice

Sendak loses himself in the evocation of folds in clothes. Ida's clothes and her mother's clothes are lovingly portrayed as a mass of shadowy folds, as out of Renaissance painters such as Michelangelo Merisi da Caravaggio or Fra Filippo Lippi. As Ida's predicament worsens, her rain cloak become filled with more lines and folds.[3] Renaissance artists used folds in exactly the same dramatic manner, to evoke the psychological aspects of the figures.

Ida's yellow rain cloak is a modern version of the magical cloak or clothing of traditional fairy tales, such as the Little Red Riding Hood's cloak, or the cloak of invisibility in *Twelve Dancing Princesses*. Ida's mother's cloak helps her to become invisible in Maurice Sendak's favourite fashion – by flying.

Outside Over There is full of art historical references, if you want to take note of them. This art historical dimension is one of the levels Maurice Sendak spoke about. For instance, in the picture where Wolfgang Amadeus Mozart appears, there is a pastoral, sylvan evocation, complete with distant green hills dotted with trees, a river meandering in the foreground to middle distance, an 18th century bridge and masses of foliage out of the art of Claude Lorrain. The illustration of Ida and her mother standing on the rocks looking out to sea recalls J.M.W. Turner's seascapes and pictures of harbours, which themselves drew on the Dutch 17th and 18th century painters.

Outside Over There is a circular narrative, like *Where the Wild Thing Are, In the Night Kitchen* and *Dear Mili*. Ida ends up where she left off: the first and last pictures depict a single action, a baby's step.[4] Max ends up in his bedroom again; the child in *Dear Mili* returns to her homeland; in *In the Night Night Kitchen* Mickey ends up in bed again.

There are many delights in *Outside Over There*. The colouring throughout, for instance, which is soft and luminous. Ida is particularly powerfully depicted. She is a quite different protagonist from *Wild Things* Max and *Night Kitchen* Mickey. She is just as resourceful as them, as any fairy tale heroine.

She moves through the emotions of bravery, anger, affection and duty. She is a dynamic character, swift in her bare feet.

Maurice Sendak emphasizes her dynamism in a number of pictures. When Ida blows her wonderhorn, for instance, she is shown in a ballet dancer's pose: she leans her weight on her left foot, leaning onto her knee; the other foot is stretched out and pointing; she holds the wonderhorn in her left hand and blows it, while her right hand, held outstretched, helps to balance her. With her head tilted down and her eyes fixed on some distant goal, Ida is clearly someone in control of her destiny. She looks relaxed yet dignified, she is poised and ready to fulfil her duties. (Sendak had some models pose for photographs, for the first time in his career, to get the drawings right, and it certainly paid off).

As soon as Ida blows the wonderhorn, in the midst of the goblins, she assumes a huge scale, her head touching the top and her feet touching the bottom of the pictures. With her legs planted firmly apart, Ida, in her blue dress, becomes a strong pyramid shape, contrasting with the rounded, tubby baby goblins. In the third picture of the goblins dancing, where they are dissolving into a 'dancing stream', Ida is shown so large that she has to bend down to fit into the picture frame (like Alice in the White Rabbit's house).

Ida is portrayed with a tremendous gestural verve: hugging the changeling baby, or shaking her fists at the goblins, or seen falling out of the window, or dancing and blowing the wonder-horn. Ida is as active as the most dynamic Maurice Sendak character, Mickey from *In the Night Kitchen.*

The cover for *Outside Over There* shows the two main characters in the garden near the house, surrounded by a white fence and sunflowers. Ida is seen protecting the baby, again assuming a dynamic stance, hand on her knee, bending to one side, holding the wonderhorn. The baby is pointing, and Ida follows her gaze: maybe they are looking toward the land of 'outside over there', or perhaps they see the goblins approaching.

Maurice Sendak seems to have been very inspired at this time, and had pictures in abundance for *Outside Over There*, for not only does the title page get an illustration, as with his earlier books, but the half-title page and the dedication page ('for Barbara Brooks') are also graced with illustrations. Thus, before the story proper starts with the words 'When Papa was away at sea', the reader has seen four pictures of Ida and the baby. In three of these pictures, the goblins are seen, carrying ladders, holding the wonderhorn, or chasing Ida and her sister. The first double-page spread, of Mama in the arbor, also contains goblins carrying a ladder, with the child crying.

The next six pictures are all based in the elegant 18th century interior of Ida's house. Ida charms the sunflowers through the window with the wonderhorn while the child stares – Maurice Sendak has skillfully captured the look of wonder on a baby's face (not easy). In the second interior, the sky darkens as if before a storm. The potentially worrying image of the goblins kidnapping the baby is off-set by the comic wide-eyed stare of the changeling. In the next pictures, in the window we see Ida's father's sailing ship on choppy seas, then sinking in a storm. The lightning and thunder, the raging sea, the sunflowers bursting through the window, all exaggerate Ida's anger.

The ocean scene in the following pictures alternates between stormy and relatively calm – again one thinks of 18th century watercolour paintings (such as John Sell Cotman or Thomas Girtin) in Maurice Sendak's seascapes. The next series of double-page spreads depicts Ida's flight to the secondary world of 'outside over there', and Sendak's illuminating device of showing a number of different scenes within the same unified space. On the far left, a full moon is obscured by storm clouds. This group of white and grey billowing clouds and brilliant full moon is a feature of most of the following illustrations. Sendak introduces the device of the underground cave in the next pictures, where Ida is seen looking directly at the viewer as she flies over the nighttime world. Papa's ship is seen again, in the distance.

The central picture shows Ida floating, goblins guarding the caves, the baby sitting on its own in a cave, two sailors staring at the viewer, a ruined castle on a hill (which looks a lot like Corfe Castle in Dorset, U.K.), Mama in the arbor, a shepherd sleeping beside his flock of sheep, and the full moon amidst enormous clouds. This is one of Maurice Sendak's busiest and most complex illustrations, but the large size of the double-page spread enables him to position each sub-scene within the larger scene. In this spectacular illustration, Sailor Papa's song is shown in its own caption box, a device that is repeated at the end and the beginning of the 1981 book. It is significant that Ida receives inspiration from her father not her mother at this crucial point.

The full moon and grandiose cloudscapes are not jettisoned when Maurice Sendak moves the narrative into the goblins' underground caves. Though the viewer sees rocky roofs at each side of the goblins' caves, most of the backgrounds consist of an epic sky, the sort seen in John Martin's Biblical visions (such as his *Apocalypse* trilogy of the 1850s). When Ida falls into the goblins' wedding scene, the observer sees the full moon on the right, and the father's ship, now in calmer waters. But behind the goblins and Ida is another source of light, which is best described as heavenly.

The next illustration again features the full moon, clouds, sea and ship on the right, and the visionary, heavenly light in the centre. While incidents of a seemingly domestic nature occur in the foreground (images of children dancing), the background is complex and visionary. There are two magical light sources for a start: the full moon, prime illuminator of all things occult, witchy and supernatural, and the celestial luminescence. When the goblins are seen dancing and disappearing into a stream/ steam, the source of Ida's magic is seen: the boiling clouds and heavenly light merge into the dancing stream around the goblins. The image emphasizes the watery motifs: on the right, the seascape comes right up to the entrance to the caves, the ripples reflecting the moonlight; on the left, a waterfall is glimpsed in a forest.

In the following picture, showing the baby in the eggshell, the background scene becomes relatively naturalistic again, with the moon seen in a clear patch of sky over the sea. The final four pictures normalize the mystery and dancing frenzy of the 'outside over there' scenes. Wolfgang Mozart is depicted plinking on a keyboard in a summerhouse; the shepherd walks with his sheep on a perfect summer's day; Ida carries the child over soft moss in the forest while butterflies gleefully cavort. This illustration alone would be enough to re-centre the emotional trajectory of the narrative back to an Arcadian tranquillity, but Maurice Sendak provides four pictures (not just one) of the return to the homeland and the mother. There are two pictures, for example, showing Ida's return to her mother, where one would have sufficed. The extra (penultimate) picture allows for Sailor Papa's words to be placed in a caption box. The final picture replays the first four pictures, showing Ida holding the child's hand as she takes her first steps (though this time there are no goblins about).

Outside Over There depicts the classic mythic narrative of a descent and return, luxuriously spending as much time on the return to tranquillity and the mother-world, as on the flight and confrontation (different narrative forms, such as cinema and television, usually spend far less time on the return, the happy ending and the *dénouement*).

IX

Dear Mili

PERHAPS THE MOST haunting – and 'grown up' – of Maurice Sendak's illustrated books for younger readers is *Dear Mili* (1988). The story is a lost Brothers Grimm fairy tale, discovered in 1983. As with *Where the Wild Things Are* or *Outside Over There* (which it most resembles), no amount of explanation will account for the haunting quality of *Dear Mili*. (A further link with *Outside Over There* is the dedication of *Dear Mili* – 'For my sister, Natalie'; *Outside Over There* was very much concerned with Sendak's sister. *Dear Mili* is in some respects a sequel, and companion book – there are further narrative affinities, such as a girl undertaking a journey, the father who's away, similar mother figures).

First of all, the story is from the Grimms (in this case, Wilhelm Grimm), which means we are more in the realm of the sober *Juniper Tree* than the exuberant picture book style of *In the Night Kitchen*. However, unlike *The Juniper Tree*, *Dear Mili* is a picture book format, and not, like *The Juniper Tree*, a small hardback book. *Dear Mili,* then, must be seen as both a picture book, the kind that Maurice Sendak is rightly famous for, and a 'serious' or 'grown up' fairy tale book. Sendak seems to be assuming, as he did with *The Juniper Tree*, that the reader of fairy tales is an adult, as well as a child. Indeed, fairy tales were originally a part of adult (oral) culture not, as in the Victorian era, often dressed up for children. Fairy tales were always written by adults and for adults.

Maurice Sendak, among other authors, loathes the idea of

fairy tales as the stuff of silly, giggly, twee, sentimental culture, the kind of art served up by adults who think that's what children want (or should have). Sendak prefers to acknowledge the serious side of children's desires, needs and anxieties. His *Dear Mili*, then, is, like *The Juniper Tree* and *Outside Over There*, a grown-up fairy tale for grown ups. Sendak's illustrations in *Dear Mili* are bright and clear enough for even children as young as three to enjoy (and understand) them, but they also speak to parents and adults.

The cover depicts the two chief protagonists, a young girl and her mother. The picture could be out of *Outside Over There*. It presents an idealized pastoral world of enthralling beauty: the waterfall, the rose bush in full bloom, the sunlit glade in the woods. However, this is the most uncomplicated illustration in *Dear Mili*: all the others contain contradictions and anxiety.

The opening picture shows an image of a domestic idyll in the countryside. Although the protagonists seem to be happy with their lot, sitting outside their little cottage, all is not well. For a start, as the golden leaves show, it is not high Summer, as in the usual fairy tale, but well into Fall. Secondly, although the (guardian) angel is there, nestling in the trees behind the two women, his presence cannot prevent the oncoming conflagration. One of the dogs looks up and in the sky there is a billowing grey cloud, which's turning orange at the edges. At first this golden cloud seems like a late afternoon scene, the sort of sky that Nicolas Poussin loved to paint (as in his *Bacchanals, Triumphs* and revels based on Ovid's *Metamorphoses*).

The tender scene of maternal bliss in the first picture, with the young mother caressing her daughter's hair, is completely overturned in the second illustration. Here Maurice Sendak depicts war as an enormous fire raging in Heaven. The flames lick around the edges of each black cloud (the yellow-edged clouds also look like sunflowers); one of the dogs hides the table; the angel covers his eyes; the child cowers in the folds of her mother's dress. This is one of the most dramatic changes from one picture to the next in Maurice Sendak's *œuvre*. With this disaster, the child must leave the homestead: thus far the fairy tale is a classic narrative, displaying a contented world which's torn apart, creating the need for the journey. A thousand books and movies about the Second World War offer exactly the same narrative line: equilibrium then the oncoming slaughter (the group of children standing in a church's ruins in one of the pictures is derived from a photo from Izieu, France, of children before they were taken to Auschwitz).

The next stage in *Dear Mili* involves the classic device of the young child entering the forest. The third picture shows the child being told to leave by her mother: the configuration of child on the left and the mother on the right will be echoed in the final, heart-rending picture. The forest in the fourth picture is a far more inhospitable place than the magical forest that grows in Max's room in *Where the Wild Things Are.* With gnarled and hollow trunks and twisted branches, it is an archetypal fairy tale forest. The presence of a large black raven adds to the sense of foreboding.

The text of *Dear Mili* at this point indicates the typical contents of a fairy tale wood: wild beasts, crows, wind, a storm. The fifth picture is the first double-page spread. The forest extends on all sides around the forlorn girl (though her guardian angel still keeps her company). The oddest element of this picture, though, is the group of peasants with sticks trudging over a wooden bridge. They are haggard figures, looking Eastern European or Russian, a little like prisoners of war; behind them looms a large grey building: a factory, perhaps, or, more ominously, a (military) prison.

After this, the illustrations brighten. The sixth picture in Maurice Sendak's *Dear Mili* shows the lost girl sitting down again, but on the edge of the forest (there is a wood meadow behind her). The picture shows that she has 'come through' the experience of being lost and alone. Here is the rose bush of the cover of the book, a huge tree with enormous flowers that dominates the picture in greens and pinks. At the foot of the rose bush is the child's guardian angel. It is the reader's first close look at him: a blue-eyed, yellow-haired youth, clearly a descendant of the Italian Renaissance cherub. The proximity of the guardian angel to the rose tree indicates where he gets his power from: the Earth, nature, the world. God is often invoked by the child as she wanders through the world.

The seventh picture portrays another classic fairy tale scene: the hut or house in the woods, with a light in the window. This hut is the destination of the child, what she has been unconsciously aiming for. Wilhelm Grimm's text sign-posts the divine nature of the appearance of the house at this point:

> *Then one by one the stars came out, and looking up at them the child said: "How bright are the nails on the great door of Heaven! What a joy it will be when God opens it!" Then suddenly a star seemed to have fallen to the ground. As the child came nearer, the light grew bigger and bigger until at length she came to a little house and saw that the light was shining from the window.*

God appears often in this Grimm story. Here, God shows the child the way by the star of Heaven falling to Earth: it is one of a few references to the Christian story in *Dear Mili*. Indeed, the person in the haven is no less a figure than St Joseph, the personage who, the text tells the reader, 'long ago had cared for the Christ Child here on earth' (24). The old man is essentially an archetypal magician-hermit type, with his monk's garb and Merlinesque white beard (the story is from Grimm, remember, not Sendak, who doesn't usually refer to God in his texts, but Grimms often did).

In Renaissance paintings – for instance, of the *Nativity* or *The Rest on the Flight Into Egypt* (by, say, Gerard David, Robert Campin or Giovanni Bellini) – Joseph is always depicted as an old man, an onlooker, forever exiled to the periphery. The focus is always on the Madonna and Child.

The eighth picture in *Dear Mili*, of St Joseph and the child in his hut, is theatrical: the hut is shown open on one side, like a stage set (and also like the cowshed in which Jesus lies in the manger in Nativity scenes). In amongst the Biblical allusions, are typical Sendakian ones: the moon outside the window from *Where the Wild Things Are*, the dog, the neatly dressed child from *Outside Over There.* This is the happiest point in the story, when the child lives most of her life, and the subsequent pictures depict that happiness. The colours of the first picture, in which the child was existing in rural bliss with her mother (reds, yellows, oranges) return, and are deepened.

The middle pictures are the richest in *Dear Mili*, associated with the child's experience of living with the old man, eating frugally but feeling full up, enjoying the birds singing and beautiful flowers. Maurice Sendak plays with scale, enlarging the flowers, so they are enormous, several feet across. The second picture of the child's stay with St Joseph (picture number nine) blooms into reds and yellows, dramatically contrasting with the cool blues and greys and muted pinks of the preceding moonlit image. Around the woodland hut grow giant flowers, including the sunflowers which had been seen in the second (war) picture.

The tenth picture in *Dear Mili* marks one of the highpoints of the child's idyll with St Joseph, with the child shown touching a huge flower. Behind her grows a massive red rose, from the rose tree of the cover and sixth picture. The presence and abundance of the flowers in this part of the story stand, obviously, for the child's paradisal life. The flowers also offer a distinctly feminine presence: in this tenth picture, the gigantic red and pink petals surround the child on all sides. Her mother is still with her, as the ring of flowers around her shows. She is surrounded by pink and red, and this colour is associated in *Dear Mili* with the mother. In picture ten, Joseph is shown in blues and greys, staring off into the distance.

Then perhaps comes the oddest part of the story, the

appearance of the twin girl. Only now does the disappearance of the guardian angel from the St Joseph pictures become clear: with St Joseph, the girl was safe (although she had to do most of the work around the house, such as providing food, for herself, a traditional aspect of fairy tales – work, work, work). The twelfth picture is the second double-page illustration of *Dear Mili*: flowers still predominate. Ten or so roses surround the sombre figure of St Joseph, as is apposite for this (Christian) side of the story. A gigantic spray of red flowers divides Joseph from the twin children, who walk away from him, towards their own part of the forest. This picture shows the child growing away from Joseph and towards her companion.

The Eastern European allusions in Maurice Sendak's Grimm story appear in this second double-page picture, as they did in the first double-page illustration. Behind Joseph are the ruins of a church and, in the distance, the sort of town house that might be seen in Prague. A group of children are shown under a tree. On the right, the wood the twins are entering is also part of a cemetery: there are Hebraic inscriptions on the tombstones: again, this could be a corner of Prague (the Jewish quarter and synagogue).

The last three pictures of *Dear Mili* depict the child's journey back to her mother. These pictures echo, like the circular narrative, the first pictures. In the thirteenth picture, which shows St Joseph's hut again, the mists of time seem to be invading the house itself. Clouds billow down from the sky into the hut. The moon behind Joseph has changed from a crescent to full. The hut looks bare and weathered: gone are the flowers erupting around the walls, and the roof has holes in it (presaging the house in the final picture). Joseph offers the child the red rose, the flower associated with the child's mother, with the guardian angel, and with the Christian subtext of the story. As Joseph says ominously: 'When this rose blooms, you will be with me again' (32).

The penultimate picture of *Dear Mili* revisits the forest that lies between Joseph's hut and the child's mother's homeland. The woodland is now tamed, no longer the life-threatening place of the fourth, crow-dominated illustration. Flowers act magically again, reviving the child when some red wine is poured into them. As expected, Sendak depicts the bindweed flowers in the foreground.

Then comes Maurice Sendak's great technique of having two pages of text on its own. Thus far in *Dear Mili* the reader has been offered luxurious pen, ink and watercolour illustrations, with many glowing colours to languish in. Then come the two pages of black-and-white writing, a sudden withdrawal of colour and imagery. This break in the illustrations is clearly to prepare for the final image, to make it even more astonishing. The story relates the tragic homecoming, the altered homeland, the new people. The war has not killed the land, though: 'All was peaceful, the grain waved in the breeze, the meadows were green, the trees were laden with fruit.' (36) This abundance connects with the paradise the child had known with St Joseph. This description of fruitfulness accentuates the shock of the child seeing her mother, now an old woman.

The story puts it poignantly enough, but Maurice Sendak's final illustration in *Dear Mili* communicates it magnificently. The picture pivots not around the giant fruit-bearing tree in the middle foreground, with its scarlet, green, golden and yellow leaves; not on the huge setting sun; not on the new moon in the cloudy, grey sky; not on the ruined church on the left; not on the dilapidated house on the right; not on the child carrying the red rose; but on the mother, wrinkled, bent, her eyes closed with age, exhaustion, and grief, her bony fingers and arms stretched out towards the child in a poignant gesture of acceptance and yearning.

What a finale to a great book! Maurice Sendak excels himself with this picture, this book. While *Where the Wild Things Are* and *In the Night Kitchen* had startled with their bold, energetic images, and *Outside Over There* had enchanted with its soft pastel colours and magical adventures, *Dear Mili* moves into a deeper, more tragic realm. The mother stretching her hands is a sorrowful image, contrasting piquantly with the first picture in the book, where the young, smiling mother had negligently caressed her child's hair. Now they are separated, and all the yearning for the meeting comes from the time-worn mother. The child looks no different. (Time passing in the outside world but not in some magical realm is a common motif in fairy tales).

The final picture is full of Autumnal colours and imagery – the tree with its Fall colours and fruit, the setting sun – but as the picture is read from right to left, the sky and landscape darkens to greys and purples. To, in short, death. The final picture in *Dear Mili* is not the end of the book: there is one more page, the final paragraph, with its haunting mixture of magic and Christianity, tenderness and redemption:

> *All evening they sat happily together. Then they went to bed calmly and cheerfully, and next morning the neighbours found them dead. They had fallen happily asleep, and between them lay Saint Joseph's rose in full bloom.* (40)

It is not a traditional wedding at the end of this fairy tale, then, with the hero/ine revealed to be the loyal, hard-working and kind person s/he always was, nor the good riddance of the baddie, and the recovery of the pot of gold, but the death of the two main protagonists. It works, though, because of the sense of (Christian) transcendence that is alluded to throughout the story. The child has led, in the end, a happy life; though the mother's life has been one of hardship, she too gains her last wish: to see her child again. By the magic of fairy tales the years of loss, suffering and separation are swept away, and healed.

X

Maurice Sendak's Other Books

ONE WOULDN'T HAVE known Maurice Sendak was destined for the greatness of *Where the Wild Things Are* by looking at his early illustrations. Sendak's early paintings and drawings show a competent artist at work, but nothing exceptional. The early self-portraits reveal an artist grappling with the basic rules of art. The early Sendak children, in *A Hole to Dig* (1952) and *Charlotte and the White Horse* (1955), are not anywhere near the accomplished depictions of children and babies in *Outside Over There* and *In the Night Kitchen.* The illustrations to *Seven Tales* (1959), from Hans Christian Andersen, are particularly flat and disappointing; but in *The Juniper Tree* Sendak demonstrated he had mastered the East European backgrounds and complex characters necessary for illustrating fairy tales in the classic 19th century manner. Sendak has also illustrated Wilhelm Hauff, Clemens Brentano, Herman Melville, Heinrich von Kleist, and George MacDonald (*The Golden Key* and *The Light Princess*).

Maurice Sendak's 3D wooden toys depicting *Old Mother Hubbard, Hansel and Gretel, Miss Muffet* and *Little Red Riding Hood* (made with his brother Jack in 1948) are more like the quirky, humorous Sendak readers recognize. In the *Little Red Riding Hood* mechanical toy, the girl faints and falls over when the wolf pops his head out of the bed clothes.

THE MOON JUMPERS

MAURICE SENDAK'S *The Moon Jumpers* (1959) is an intriguing book (the story is by Janice May Udry). The plot has that element of strangeness dear to Sendak. Sendak does not now find *The Moon Jumpers* one of his favourite books, but it has something of the haunting quality which he tries to evoke in most of his work.

The Moon Jumpers is about children who dance under the moon. That alone would be enough to intrigue Maurice Sendak. The black-and-white drawings, it's true, are not Sendak's best. They are sub-Ardizzone works, which Sendak would not allow into picture books after he had developed his mature style from *Where the Wild Things Are* onwards. But the purple, green and blue washes in the colour illustrations confer a suitably magical atmosphere on the proceedings. The soft washes were also used to poetic effect in *Mr Rabbit and the Lovely Present* (by Charlotte Zolotow, 1962) and the wistful images in 1956's *I Want To Paint My Bathroom Blue.* The figures are all movement, bending, stretching, waving to the moon. The Queen of the Night is of course a full, round, brilliant moon. It is shown as the instigator of the night's revelries.

Maurice Sendak's pictures depict children having a wild time at night, on their own, dancing barefoot and very carefree. The three central two-page colour pictures in *The Moon Jumpers* show the revelry at its height; in the first picture, the children throw their arms in the air like ballet dancers; in the second, they are doing handstands on the flower-sprinkled grass; in the third, most fully worked picture, the children are seen gesturing to the moon. This image looks forward to the rumpus of *Where the Wild Things Are.* It also features those moonlit spaces, where paths lead off into the dark forest, that became one of Sendak's recurring motifs, used widely in *Outside Over There.*

Maurice Sendak's pictures for *Mr Rabbit and the Lovely*

Present were called 'luminescent' by one critic (D. Klemin, 63) and 'impressionist' by another (P. Nodelman, 89). Sendak's pictures give out an aura of calm and nostalgia. 'Wistful' seems accurate, as with *The Moon Jumpers.*

KENNY'S WINDOW

THE IDEA OF CHILDREN staying up all night without going to bed lies behind much of Maurice Sendak's work, from *Kenny's Window* through *Where the Wild Things Are* to *In the Night Kitchen. Kenny's Window* (1956) was the first book that Sendak wrote and illustrated. If Kenny manages to answer seven questions he can live in a magic place where he will never have to go to bed. The questions are riddles, such as:

> *What looks inside and what looks outside? ...Can you hear a horse on the roof? ...Do you always want what you think you want?*

Kenny's Window, like so much of Maurice Sendak's work, has a wistful melancholy behind it. An example of this is the scene where Kenny sits up in his bed looking out of his window at the full moon. This is clearly a primal scene in Sendak's art. The child looking out of the window yearningly replays a fundamental emotion in Sendak's work. The moon, preferably full, spins Sendak's characters back to some primal moment. Indeed, as an object and symbol there is nothing to beat the moon for sheer power – in witchcraft, in Classic mythology, in alchemy, in poetry, the moon is supremely the manifestation of otherness, occultism, and the powers of the night.

> *I love full moons. It was my old friend Tomi Ungerer who pointed out to me that my books are full of discrepancies* [commented Sendak]. *Full moons go to three-quarters and even halves without reason. But the moon appears in my*

books for graphic, not astronomical, reasons – I simply must have that shape on the page. (in AMS, 93)

Although the moon is a powerful source of light in Maurice Sendak's pictures, it is not the only source. Sendak invents light sources which do not have a 'realistic' basis. For instance, in *Outside Over There* a shadow is cast from a table leg from the light from the window; when the sky darkens outside, the shadow is still there, adding to the dreamlike quality of the narrative.[1] In *Where the Wild Things Are* the moon changes, sometimes misty, sometimes a crescent, sometimes full, now near the vanishing point, now exactly on it. Each change modifies the emotional impact of the pictures. An equivalence is conjured between Max's white wolf suit and the whiteness of the full moon as the forest appears in his room. The moon grows increasingly dominant, until Max stands in the moonlit and mysterious forest. The continuity between Max, the wolf suit, the moon and the Land of the Wild Things is very clear. Here the wolf connotes wildness, otherness, the primitive and animal, while the moon has for æons presided over all things occult, unknown, magical, religious and mysterious.

BEE-MAN, BAT-POET, FIELDMOUSE AND OTHER ANIMALS

ILLUSTRATIONS TO WORKS of the 1960s, such as *The Bat-Poet* and *Pleasant Fieldmouse,* revealed Maurice Sendak adopting his trusted black-and-white pen-and-ink technique, which gave the illustrations the darkness of 19th century etchings. In *Pleasant Fieldmouse* (by Jan Wahl, 1964), Sendak drew landscapes in black-and-white which recall, in their better moments, some of the Old Masters such as Rembrandt van Rijn or Martin Schongauer in their etchings and drawings. Sendak is a historically-aware artist. *The Animal Family* (1965) – also, like *The Bat-Poet* (1964), by Randall Jarrell –

contained an image straight out of J.M.W. Turner, of a sunset. The viewer looks directly into a sun low in the sky over a seascape. In his illustrations for other writers' work one sees Sendak alternating between his three or so styles: *The Bee-Man of Orn* (by Frank Stockton, 1964) and *Lullabies and Night Songs* (by Alec Wilder, 1965) are painted with pastel-hued watercolours, looking like Thomas Rowlandson and other 18th century illustrators.

The illustrations to *Lullabies and Night Songs* are deliberately loose, using broken colour. In *Bee-Man of Orn* Maurice Sendak drew a large dragon with red wings. Between its huge paws is a Sendakian motif, a weeping baby, complete with old-style bonnet. The light touch of the pastel-hued illustrations in *The Bee-Man of Orn* looks forward to Sendak's most accomplished work as a picture book illustrator, *Outside Over There* and *Dear Mili.*

The Bat-Poet, Pleasant Fieldmouse, Zlateh the Goat and Other Stories (by I.B. Singer, 1966), *The Animal Family* (1965), *The Golden Key* (by George MacDonald, 1967), *Higglety Pigglety Pop!* (1967), *A Kiss For Little Bear* (by Else Minarik, 1968), and *The Light Princess* (by George MacDonald, 1969) used a black-and-white pen-and-ink technique. The black-and-white pen-and-ink style is part of Maurice Sendak's trademark. He has employed it throughout his career. It has a timeless quality. It is less prone to changing fashions as is colour reproduction. Sendak employed the black-and-white pen-and-ink in early works, such as *Circus Girl* (by Jack Sendak, 1957) and in later works such as *Fly By Night* (1976). The cover for *Lullabies and Night Songs* used bold watercolours and pen-and-ink, in a style familiar from *In the Night Kitchen.*

Maurice Sendak's more 'cartoon-like' illustrations, which do not use crosshatching or fine detail, include the 1958 story *What Do You Say, Dear?* (by Sesyle Joslin, 1961), *She Loves Me, She Loves Me Not* (by Robert Keeshan, 1963), *How Little Lion Visited Times Square* (by Amos Vogel, 1963) and *Some*

Swell Pup (1976). Each book demands its own stylistic approach, Sendak says, but he does not regard style as significant in itself; rather, style is 'purely a means to an end' (1980, 41).

FLY BY NIGHT

FLY BY NIGHT (1976) is one of Maurice Sendak's more unusual projects (one of a number he illustrated of Randall Jarrell's books for children). Like illustrations to *The Light Princess* and *The Golden Key*, *Fly By Night* contains black-and-white drawings, very finely crafted, very finely detailed. One of the central images contains a range of Sendakian motifs, from the bonneted baby to the full moon. However, there are fantastical elements here too, such as the huge owl face with its beady eyes staring at the viewer. Like the illustrations in *Outside Over There*, this *Fly By Night* picture is very busy: on the left, two hares spring over some grass; above them, the full moon; next to the moon, some shadowy trees; below these, a mother and baby (based on Sendak's own mother and himself as a baby); around their feet are lambs; beside the lambs, a fox looks hungrily at some more sheep; behind the fox, there's a bridge and a river, with two ducks on it; some more sheep are on the bridge; along further to the right, there's a shepherdess with a crook; behind her, more trees; in the distance, the corner of a house in shade, with a light on in the window; more trees; on the horizon, there's a town, perhaps the outline of a church; floating above this nightscape is a naked boy, lying on his side, his back to the viewer; and above him, the giant owl face.

Maurice Sendak manages to include all these elements (and more) without the picture seeming crowded. Well, it *is* crowded, but it doesn't seem crowded, it does not look like a mess. This is important, for Sendak, over the years, crowds his images with more and more information, until, by the time of *The Juniper Tree*, the pictures are jammed with data, even though they are printed relatively small in size compared to (say) the pictures for *Where the Wild Things Are.*

HECTOR PROTECTOR

ONE OF MAURICE SENDAK'S most accomplished books is *Hector Protector and As I Went Over the Water* (1965), which is of the same stature as Sendak's best works – *Where the Wild Things Are, The Juniper Tree* and *Outside Over There. Hector Protector* employs Sendak's by now familiar water-colour/ pen-and-ink style, made famous in *Where the Wild Things Are,* set to a *Mother Goose* rhyme.

> *Hector Protector was dressed all in green,*
> *Hector Protector was sent to the Queen.*
> *The Queen did not like him, no more did the King,*
> *So Hector Protector was sent back again.*

The usual Sendakian motifs are there – cake, play-acting, dogs, babies, and lions. It is one of Maurice Sendak's most humorous books, drawing on one of his heroes, Randolph Caldecott (1846-86), who also invented many images to go with a short nursery rhyme. He introduces cartoon-style speech bubbles ('So!', 'Dopies!', 'No!') into a drawing style that looks back to 19th century book illustration. It is this clash of styles that helps make Sendak's art so interesting.

Hector himself is one of Maurice Sendak's spunky protagonists, decidedly angry – angry at his mother trying to squeeze him into a costume, angry with the Queen ('I hate the Queen!' he shouts), angry with the lion, angry with the king. Like Mickey, Hector is very active, kicking his legs in the air, flailing his wooden sword around, bashing the lion, twining the snake around the sword.

With *Hector Protector*, Maurice Sendak shows he is one of the most accomplished of illustrators of *Mother Goose* rhymes. His *Mother Goose* illustrations draw on the history of book illustration, and acknowledge former illustrators. At the same time Sendak establishes his *Mother Goose* as very much his own. His nursery rhyme art is at once 'old-fashioned' and new, at once traditional and up-to-date. While the drawing style evokes 19th century children's book illustration, the humour and actions of the protagonists are distinctly modern.

Hector Protector, and the companion piece *As I Went Over the Water*, shows how deft Maurice Sendak is at improvizing. The nursery rhymes are very 'simple', there seems to be little to go on for an illustrator ('As I went over the water/ The water went over me'). Sendak introduces items such as cake, a snake, a lion, crows, and a king and queen. Sendak makes them very entertaining. He clearly enjoys expanding a text from seemingly ordinary words. In *Where the Wild Things Are* the text does not give much indication of the emotional state of the participants (the text says baldly 'he was sad'). Look at the pictures, though, and the emotions become very clear. Significantly, folk tales were originally oral tales, which were told 'before ever they were printed and they carry within themselves all the illustration that they need', noted B. Alderson in *Looking at Picture Books* (37).

The sense of improvization and spontaneity is very apparent from Maurice Sendak's work, where the action never stops. In *Hector Protector*, the World Mother Goose Theatre production in *Higglety Pigglety Pop!* and *In the Night Kitchen,* the action is continuous. Like a silent comedy movie, Sendak's narratives move swiftly from one caper to the next, from one joke to another, from one set-up to another. *Hector Protector* and *In the Night Kitchen* are full of action, like the films of Laurel and Hardy, Buster Keaton, Charlie Chaplin and the Marx Brothers.

HIGGLETY PIGGLETY POP!

HIGGLETY PIGGLETY POP! (1967) brilliantly shows off Maurice Sendak's sense of narration, plot, continuity, sequentiality, time and meaning. *Higglety Pigglety Pop!* features a staging of a theatrical production, as in *Hector Protector.* The 'World Mother Goose Theatre' production incorporates two of Sendak's favourite themes: *Mother Goose* rhymes and lively 'animation' or narration. Sendak dexterously illustrates the nursery rhyme 'Higglety Pigglety Pop!' with a mock-up of a 19th century toy theatre (mock 'classical' pillars each side of the stage, a curtain with tassels above, a woman in Victorian costume).

The space, as in the Grimm illustrations, is very compact, with the characters – a lion, a dog, a woman, a cat – squashed into it. The woman and the dog are drawn to scale, but when the lion arrives, he's huge. Each little square black-and-white picture in the 'World Mother Goose Theatre' show of *Higglety Pigglety Pop!* has a bubble with one phrase written in it taken from the nursery rhyme: 'in a flurry' or 'pigglety'.

Maurice Sendak's *Higglety Pigglety Pop!* is an outstanding visualization of a nursery rhyme. It shows just how much an illustrator can develop a theme from a seemingly simple and banal beginning (just 22 words):

Higglety Pigglety Pop!
The dog has eaten the mop!
The pig's in a hurry,
The cat's in a flurry,
Higglety Pigglety Pop!

Maurice Sendak shows that it is still possible to do new things with old material such as nursery rhymes. Sendak demonstrates that children's book illustration still has a long way to develop. After all, it has a relatively short history (from the 18th century onwards, say) compared to Western painting, which goes back hundreds of years to mediæval times (or thousands if one counts cave paintings such as Lascaux).

KING GRISLY-BEARD

AT THE SAME TIME as *The Juniper Tree* (1973), Maurice Sendak produced *King Grisly-Beard*, 'a tale from the Brothers Grimm'. Unlike the illustrations for *The Juniper Tree*, Sendak's pictures for *King Grisly-Beard* are in his light style, as found in *Some Swell Pup, Hector Protector* and *Where the Wild Things Are*. Like *Some Swell Pup*, there is a father figure here, called 'the impresario' (a self-portrait of Sendak), and two children, a girl and a boy. As with *Some Swell Pup*, the tone is light-hearted and humorous. *King Grisly-Beard* is introduced as a piece of play-acting or theatre. In front of the half-title page is a picture of the two children in modern, American clothes. On the half-title spread, the two children are seen approaching the behatted 'impresario', who holds a poster saying

> *WANTED! Extraordinary actor & actress to play leading roles in Wilhelm & Jacob Grimms' fabulous King Grisly-Beard, inquire within.*

There are a number of layers to Maurice Sendak's Grimm story, then:

(1) There is the playacting of the two American children. Maurice Sendak reminds the reader that this is play-acting, because before page one is reached, where the tale starts, we have seen four pictures (in *Outside Over There* and *In the Night Kitchen* Sendak also introduced a number of illustrations before the beginning of the narrative).

(2) There is the text of the tale itself, as translated by Edgar Taylor (the translator of the first important editions of the Grimms in English),[2] which tells one narrative.

(3) Underneath the printed words are Sendak's colour

pictures, which illustrate certain moments from the written text.

(4) Maurice Sendak has added speech to these pictures, however, providing another layer of meanings. Like Mickey in *In the Night Kitchen,* the people in *King Grisly-Beard* exclaim in small speech bubbles. They say, 'Oh!', 'Yip', 'Ah', 'Wow!' and 'Feh'. These are the sort of paralinguistic noises one sees in comics such as *Beano* and *Dandy*: 'hur hur' for someone laughing, 'tsk' for someone tetchily tutting.

Maurice Sendak, then, adds a lot to the Grimms' story of *King Grisly-Beard.* He turns it into a comicbook-like tale, where the princess, played by the American child, points at the line of assembled potential suitors and cries 'Wallface!' or 'Dumpling!'. Sendak transforms the tale into a humorous piece, though there are few images of people smiling.

The 'seriousness' or 'darkness' of the fairy tale in *King Grisly-Beard*, then, is not completely swept away by Maurice Sendak's comicbook treatment. *King Grisly-Beard* is a counterpoint to the far more 'serious' and 'dark' pictures in *The Juniper Tree.* In the latter book, Sendak choose one moment to illustrate, one moment which summed up the fairy tale, while in *King Grisly-Beard* there are (in total) twenty pictures. Although the tone is intended to be light in *King Grisly-Beard*, the darkness creeps in. The tale, as with so many of the Grimms' stories, features extreme poverty. Though Sendak's pictures are humorous, they do not shy away from the bleaker aspects of the story.

SOME SWELL PUP

SOME SWELL PUP (1976) foregrounds Maurice Sendak's love of dogs in another luminous series of pictures. Here, Sendak develops the comicbook format of *In the Night Kitchen*, which integrated words and pictures in a comicbook style. Like

Raymond Briggs' *The Snowman*, *Some Swell Pup* splits the page up into little pictures. Like comic strips, there are speech balloons. The arrival of the dog in *Some Swell Pup* signals the start of a series of funny and ridiculous situations for the girl and boy heroes. The dog's antics are but a pretext for the conflicting desires of the children. They each try to possess the dog in their own way, using their own language and gestures. The dog becomes the central component in an emotional tug of war, just like a child in a divorce case.

The book is about the socialization of young people, via the means of relating to a pet. Here, the pain of relating to another individual is detailed at each stage in the social process. Huge gaps that were leapt over in previous Maurice Sendak books (the stages of Max's rage in the early part of *Where the Wild Things Are*, for instance) are described in detail.

Visually, *Some Swell Pup* is a cross between *In the Night Kitchen* and the lighter style as used in books such as *Lullabies and Night Songs*. As with *In the Night Kitchen*, *Some Swell Pup* is infused with bright colours, bright reds, yellows, light blues. There are some 87 pictures in *Some Swell Pup*, which is a very large amount for a Maurice Sendak picture book.

Maurice Sendak is inventive with his use of space and layout. He uses a base of six small pictures per page, but sometimes has one picture across two columns, sometimes three wide pictures over two columns, or two large pictures, sometimes he takes away the background, as when the children are in the wood looking for the pup, and on a few occasions he has just one large picture per page.

As with *King Grisly Beard*, the story of *Some Swell Pup* starts well before page one. There are pictures on the half-title page, the title page, the dedication page ('for Connie, Erda, lo, and Aggie') and the imprint page. Two central illustrations in *Some Swell Pup* depart from the comicbook style, to depict the dreams of the boy and the girl. Here Maurice Sendak's more mature style is employed, though still with bright bold colour (yellows, reds, blues). The dream pictures feature two of Sendak's motifs, dogs and large scale creatures. The dog recalls the enormous animal with eyes as big as saucers in *The Tinder-Box* by Hans Christian Andersen (although Sendak's dogs are friendly).

OTHER BOOKS

THE PROTAGONIST IN *The Sign at Rosie's Door* (1960) is the first of Maurice Sendak's feisty characters. In the early books, Sendak's humour was not so obvious. In the middle-period works, such as *The Nutshell Library, Pierre* and *Where the Wild Things Are*, the Sendak sense of humour flowered. *The Nutshell Library* showed Sendak having a lot of fun setting human figures next to animals (a lion, a monkey, a dog, an alligator).

Always good at monsters (it's one of the requirements for a children's book illustrator), Maurice Sendak's illustrations to Clemens Brentano's *Schoolmaster Whackwell's Wonderful Sons* (1962) featured a wonderful monster, the giant Snorrasper, floating with giant bat-wings above some frightened men in a boat. The illustration to *The Three Feathers,* from *The Juniper Tree*, is a huge frog, staring into the eyes of the story's protagonist.

One of Maurice Sendak's best monsters is the enormous griffin in *The Griffin and the Manor Canon* (1963). The monster coolly takes the temperature of a baby in its cot. The humorous possibilities of the contrast between the massive griffin and the baby are emphasized by the baby's facial expression of horror as it contemplates the befeathered creature looming before it. Meanwhile, the griffin quietly goes about is business, with an expression that recalls Snoopy's basic mood in the *Peanuts* cartoons.

George MacDonald's *The Light Princess* (1969) includes

archetypal Sendakian images of an open window and a baby next to it (or, in this case, a flying baby). Sendak portrays the Princess as a naked baby, but she is not a typical female nude figure.

LATER BOOKS

Later picture books by Maurice Sendak included *Brundibar* (2003), *Swine Lake* by James Marshall (1998), *What Can You Do With a Shoe?* (1997), *We Are All In the Dumps With Jack and Guy* (1993), and *The Miami Giants* by Arthur Yorinks (1995). Other books are *In Grandpa's House* (1985), *I Saw Esau* (1992), *Penthesilea* (1998), and *Bumble-Ardy* (2011).

Maurice Sendak has illustrated books about Herman Melville (*A Biography* by Hershel Parker), and by Melville (*Pierre*, 1995), another influence, *Sleep Demons* (by Bill Hayes), *A Perfect Friend* by Reynolds Price, *Dear Genius* by Ursula Nordstrom, *A Dybbuk* by S.Y. Ansky, and *Penthesilea* by Heinrich von Kleist.

The Jewish experience has always been vital in the art of Maurice Sendak, but in more recent works the artist has foregrounded it even more than usual. *In Grandpa's House* (1985) was a picture book with a 1970 text by Sendak's father, Philip (d. 1970). A *hommage* to the Old World, from the perspective of the New World, *In Grandpa's House* features black-and-white drawings in the manner of *The Juniper Tree* (though without the sense of dread and mystery of the fairy tale pictures).

A big fan of Herman Melville, Maurice Sendak illustrated a book for adults (which he'd vowed never to do [AMS2, 65]) in 1995: *Pierre*. He took a visual approach inspired by his guru, William Blake, in particular how Blake portrayed figures. The result contains plenty of nudity – perhaps more than in any other Sendak book. And not only nudity, but explicitly erotic scenarios, with figures in sexual embraces. And an emphasis on genitals (including many full male nude drawings).

The full-on approach to eroticism of *Pierre* continued with Maurice Sendak's interpretation of Heinrich von Kleist's *Penthesilea* (1998). Again, the illustrations are wildly stagey and artificial, the fruit of Sendak's work in opera, with figures crammed into the space in the style of *The Juniper Tree*, and the settings harking back to the early 19th century of *Outside Over There*.

I Saw Esau: The Schoolchild's Pocket Book (1992) was a picture book edited by Peter and Iona Opie, the influential guardians of children's literature, 'the godheads of children's books', as Sendak, a big fan of the Opies, called them (their *The Lore and Language of Schoolchildren*, for example, is a terrific study of children's nursery rhymes and sayings).

The Miami Giant (1995), by Arthur Yorinks, took up an Old World and Jewish theme for a children's story about the Mishbookers, a bunch of giants in Miami.

In 1993, Maurice Sendak published *We're All in the Dumps With Jack and Guy*, one of his very few original book texts since *Outside Over There*. Tony Kushner has suggested that *We're All in the Dumps With Jack and Guy* forms a trilogy with *Outside Over There* and *Dear Mili*. (AMS2, 33). *We're All in the Dumps With Jack and Guy* confronts hard issues such as poverty, illness, AIDS and homelessness – but using the familiar form of Sendakian children and a nursery rhyme-style text.

Swine Lake (1999), by James Marshall, was yet another children's book with a theatrical flavour (this time about a wolf who was a ballet dancer in a dance troupe of pigs – the concept might come out of Walt Disney's famous series of *Three Little Pigs* cartoons of the Thirties).

Other later Maurice Sendak projects include covers for the *New Yorker* (1993), a *Sendak In Philadelphia* show (1995), a poster for a *Dracula* centenary exhibition at the Rosenbach Museum & Library in Philly (1997), a post-9/11 poster for New

York Is Book Country (1988, 2003), a poster for the Children's Museum in Brooklyn (1998), a comic strip for *Strange Stories For Strange Kids* (2001), edited by Art Spiegelman and Françoise Mouly, a CD cover for *Stravinsky* (1996), more CD covers, and for William Shakespeare's plays (1995-96).

OTHER PROJECTS: MUSIC, OPERA, THEATRE, TELEVISION, CINEMA

IN LATER YEARS, among other projects, Maurice Sendak has produced works for musical and animated productions. Sendak is very fond of opera. In 1997, Sendak remarked:

> *To me, the best of all art forms is music and perhaps opera is my favourite, and the best best best of all that is Mozart.*

The love of music runs throughout Maurice Sendak's work for the theatre: he has often remarked how important music has been for him (and Wolfgang Amadeus Mozart above all). Clearly music sustained Sendak – knowing that his designs would be supporting some of the great works in the classical music tradition.

Maurice Sendak began working in theatre (and in particular musical theatre) in the mid-1970s, with *Where the Wild Things Are* (appropriately enough). It was an opera version with music by Oliver Knussen, to be performed by Théâtre de la Monnaie, Brussels.

By the 1980s, Maurice Sendak was deep into theatrical designs, working on Igor Stravinsky's *Renard* (Amsterdam), *The Goose of Cairo* and *Idomeneo* by Wolfgang Mozart, *L'Enfant et Les Sortileges* and *L'Heure Espagnole* by Maurice Ravel, and the two Oliver Knussen operas (AMS2, 143).

Other musical projects included the costumes and sets for *The Cunning Little Vixen* (Leos Janácek), *Love of Three Oranges* (1982, Sergei Prokofiev), *Idomeneo, Re di Creta*

(1990), *Hansel and Gretel* (1997, Engelbert Humperdinck), the ballet *Nutcracker* (1984), and *Really Rosie*, a musical production, for which he produced the sets, and a book (the show opened in Washington, DC, in October, 1980).

Perhaps Maurice Sendak's most significant works in the second half of his career have been for the stage – chiefly for opera productions, and for musical theatre. Sendak's art has always had its theatrical flourishes, but the stage designs that dominate the latter half of Sendak's career feed into all of his art – into his books and posters. The emphasis on theatricality in Sendak's art stresses the showmanship of storytelling – that telling stories means putting on a show (even if, in book form, the audience is one or two people). To keep an audience entertained for two hours you usually have to be big, loud, clear, confident, coherent, imaginative, witty, sentimental, brave. Sendak's art for opera and theatre displays that feeling for showmanship, for the razzle-dazzle of putting on a show.

For the *Where the Wild Things Are* opera (1979), Maurice Sendak created some bold set designs, expanding the original vision of the book to include frothy cloudscapes, caves, and giant close-ups of the grimacing Wild Things. *Higglety Pigglety Pop!* was also made into an opera, with music by Oliver Knussen (in 1985); both productions toured to Glyndbourne in Britain in 1985 (alongside Mozart's *Figaro* and *Cosi Fan Tutte*).

For *The Magic Flute* (1791), a 1980 opera production, Maurice Sendak revisited his beloved 18th century, clearly having a great time conjuring up the world of Wolfgang Amadeus Mozart (which had also influenced *Outside Over There*). In the opera version of *Higglety Pigglety Pop!* (1985), Maurice Sendak revisited his 1967 children's book, updating it, and expanding it considerably (Sendak contributed the *libretto*).

The Goose of Cairo (1986) was an abandoned opera by Wolfgang Amadeus Mozart, a fragment which allowed Maurice Sendak to explore Ancient Egypt yet again. In another venture in Mozartland, *Idomeneo, Re di Creta* (1990), Sendak pursued a delightfully lighthearted storybook approach, with billowing Baroque cloudscapes, Classical temple ruins, shining suns and moons, monsters and deities.

For *L'Heure Espagnole* and *L'Enfant et les Sortilèges*, by Maurice Ravel, Maurice Sendak created more of his now-familiar Old World evocations, enhanced by some delightfully OTT Art Nouveau and *fin-de-siècle* costume designs.

1997's production of Engelbert Humperdinck's opera *Hansel and Gretel* (directed, again, by Frank Corsaro, and presented at the Juilliard Theater in Gotham, and the Houston Grand Opera), was important for Maurice Sendak: it was one of his favourite fairy tales, for a start, and he fell in love with the show (his seventeenth theatrical production). Once again, Sendak mined his back catalogue – inevitably retracing his steps to his *meisterwerk*: the *Juniper Tree* Brothers Grimm book of the Seventies. Thus, the Witch from Sendak's Grimms' illustration, with her hook nose, warts, apron and bonnet, became a centrepiece.

For his opera work, you can see Maurice Sendak drawing on his panoply of symbols and motifs, time after time, and orchestrating them in new configurations: the full moons, the starry skies, the animal masks, the broken pillars, the lush vegetation, the fey princesses, the clowns, and the kings. All is over-size and dream-like, as if every set drop, background and costume design comes from a fever dream, with distances flattened onto the frontal plane, with perspectives exaggerated in Baroque *trompe l'œil* effects. Put them all together, and Sendak's musical theatre designs constitute a never-ending masquerade of 18th century Italianate culture, speckled with ancient world ingredients (usually Ancient Egypt), and some early 20th century Middle European settings.

CINEMA AND TELEVISION

The animated film *Really Rosie,* starring the *Nutshell Kids,* appeared in 1974. Maurice Sendak provided the script, song lyrics and much of the visual material (working with Carole King, a very enjoyable collaboration, he said). This was a half-hour TV special. Imagine, though, a full-length feature movie of one of Sendak's books. A few other of Sendak children's books have been animated, including *Where the Wild Things Are* and *In the Night Kitchen*; the productions are rather lacklustre, though, somewhat hollow and join-the-dots. They are also hampered by the limitations of the budget for the animation (opting to include Sendak's trademark cross-hatching presents a huge technical challenge, which the animated versions don't meet. But even the finest animation company would find that extremely difficult).

For years I imagined *Where the Wild Things Are* being given the full-blown three-years-in-the-making Walt Disney treatment, as found in the resurgence of Disney movie-making of the late 1980s onwards (*Beauty and the Beast, The Little Mermaid, Aladdin* and *The Lion King et al*). A big budget Maurice Sendak movie is a tempting prospect. All too often, however, such projects either come to nothing or wind up a mess on screen. Better, perhaps, to have Sendak remain where he works best: the picture book. (In fact, *The Wild Things* was a test for computer animation by John Lasseter (of Pixar) and animator Glen Keane (at Disney) in the early 1980s which used Sendak's book as a starting-point).

A film version of *Where the Wild Things Are* was in development at Universal for some years, before moving on to Warners, where it was planned as a live action outing with plenty of digital additions. (Dr Seuss has also had the Hollywood blockbuster treatment, with *The Grinch* in 2000 and *The Cat In the Hat* in 2003, although Hollywood had produced a wonderful film of *The 5,000 Fingers of Dr T* way back in 1951. It doesn't always work out well, though: *The Grinch* was terrific, if over-stuffed, but *The Cat In the Hat* was sadly unengaging – a case of everyone involved trying their best, but the mix not gelling out at all).

Part of the challenge of adapting short books aimed at younger readers is expanding the story into a ninety minute script. *Where the Wild Things Are*, for instance, would require huge additions to the book to make it work as a full-length movie to satisfy a global audience (Maurice Sendak commented that he hadn't been happy with Universal's take on the project. He had a contract which gave him approval of the script).

When the live-action adaption of *Where the Wild Things Are* finally appeared from Warner Brothers (in 2009), the result had barely any relation to the 1963 picture book, apart from some of the designs and incidents. It was a movie as a psychotherapy session for children *and* parents, in which Max was turned into a troubled 9 year-old – neglected, lonely, sensitive, angry. Every scene was predictable, sentimental, and crudely, bluntly psychological. The movie split audiences (however, many of the principal film critics praised it).

Cinematic equivalents with the fantasy world of Maurice Sendak would include the Czech animator Jan Svankmajer, whose dark, Gothic fantasies in stopmotion animation embody the more bizarre, wilder and more violent side of the European fairy tale: *Little Otik* (2000), *Conspirators of Pleasure* (1996), and the glorious re-interpretation of the Lewis Carroll classic in *Alice* (1988). When it comes to the surreal, the macabre and the grotesque, Svankmajer has few peers in cinema, and his *Alice* is probably the most satisfying rendition of Carroll's classic book in cinema.

The beautiful animated movies of Japanese master director Hayao Miyazaki would be equivalents of the eccentric aspects of Maurice Sendak's art. Like Sendak, Miyazaki has a vision of the world all his own, wonderfully imaginative; as a colourist he has no equal. His cinema's imbued with an extraordinary sense of space, furniture, architecture and production design, but also plenty of heart and emotion (in films such as *Spirited Away, Princess Mononoke, Howl's Moving Castle* and *Laputa: Castle in the Sky*). Miyazaki and Studio Ghibli have often drawn on the history of fairy tales and fantasy, visually and textually, like Sendak, and used classic authors as the basis for films. Like Sendak, Miyazaki has his favourite motifs which crop up in film after film: young protagonists (often girls), the moon, cats and dogs, flowers, and flight (Miyazaki's films feature the most beautiful depictions of flying in contemporary movies).

XI

Maurice Sendak and Other Illustrators

ALWAYS ONE LOOKS back to illustrators such as George Cruikshank, Randolph Caldecott and Edward Ardizzone when contemplating Maurice Sendak's art, classic book illustrators from the history of children's book illustration. Edward Ardizzone (1900-79) is an immediate predecessor in many ways. The qualities one associates with Sendak's art – tenderness and yearning, poetry and openness – are all there in Ardizzone's illustrations. Ardizzone illustrated Eleanor Farjeon, Walter de la Mare, Miguel de Cervantes, William Thackeray, Charles Dickens and William Shakespeare. Books like *Little Tim and the Brave Sea Captain* and *The Penny Fiddle* are exquisite evocations of the wonders and pains of childhood. In books such as *The Penny Fiddle* Ardizzone combines nursery rhymes and pictures in the way Sendak came to employ. Ardizzone has children impersonating the characters from the *Mother Goose* rhymes, just as Sendak did in books such as *King Grisly Beard.*

Little Tim and the Brave Sea Captain (1936), the first of Edward Ardizzone's *Little Tim* books,[1] is one of Ardizzone's most accomplished works, and it is easy to see why Maurice Sendak should admire Ardizzone so much. *Little Tim and the Brave Sea Captain* begins with a two sentence opening which starts the book with a classic narrative drive, founded on desire:

> *Little Tim lived in a house by the sea. He wanted very much to be a sailor.*

Maurice Sendak's own books have a similarly straightforward kind of text, which starts the story moving right from the outset. Ardizzone's illustrations have a lightness of touch, an openness and relaxed ease, which one can see Sendak aiming for. In almost every picture, some form of movement is suggested or depicted. Ardizzone draws delicately with a black pen and uses watercolours in a simple, direct fashion. It is a restrained form of illustration, similar to the style which Sendak employed in *Mr Rabbit and the Lovely Present* and *I Want To Paint My Bathroom Blue* (critics celebrated how Ardizzone combined drawings and text).

One can see the ancestor of Maurice Sendak's feisty protagonists (Rosie, Max, Mickey, Ida) in Little Tim, in the pictures where Tim dances on the beach crying, 'Oh I would love to', when the old boatman asks him if he'd like to lend a hand with the boat, or Tim swinging on the wire between the lifeboat and the steamer.

The charm of *Little Tim and the Brave Sea Captain* is as instantaneous as any classic children's book, but it is not so easy to pinpoint exactly what it is about Edward Ardizzone's book that is so enchanting. Ardizzone manages to capture the wholehearted leap into experience of a young boy without falling into sentimentality on one side, or cynicism on the other.

The illustrations in Edward Ardizzone's version of English fairy tales look like 19th century drawings.[2] Ardizzone keeps the images free of furniture and costume which will place the tales within any particular time zone. Ardizzone's illustrations (to tales such as *Jack and the Beanstalk, Tom Tit Tot, Cap o' Rushes* and *The Three Sillies*) are free, open ink drawings, full of verve and a vigorous, relaxed line.

✪

Children's picture books have to compete with a host of other pleasures and pursuits and visuals in the contemporary world: videos, DVDs, computers, video games, toys, television, radio, magazines, cel phones, i-Pods, cartoons, comics, cereals and food packaging, and pop music. Hence there has been a tendency since the 1970s for children's picture books to become increasingly colourful and wacky. Book publishers have explored a variety of ways of spicing up the book market, in order to provide serious competition to the myriad other leisure and entertainment activities available to children in the contemporary world.

There have been extravagant and elaborate pop-up books, books with all manner of objects attached to them (such as CDs or DVDs), books on CD-ROMS and DVDs, audio books, books which simulate computer programmes and books which emulate 'hands on' or interactive games and entertainments (the kind of interactivity found in modern museums). The reader in some recent books responds to tasks set by the text and zaps around the pages on a quest, in a multi-narrative manner.[3]

The content is often taken from superhero comics, Arthurian or Dungeons and Dragons board gaming, the familiar and widespread fusion genres of sword and sorcery/ fantasy/ horror/ science fiction. This is the children's fantasy world of *The Mighty Morphin Power Rangers, Teenage Mutant Ninja Turtles, Thunderbirds, Star Wars, Harry Potter, E.T., Jurassic Park, The Flintstones, Batman, Superman* and *Super Mario Brothers.*

Maurice Sendak has held himself aloof from such aggressive enterprises in the realm of children's literature and publishing. He has not produced pop-up, pull-out, computer-aligned, interactive or gimmicky books, the guff emerging from hyper-capitalist, market-driven and highly technological ventures. Rather, he has stuck to producing traditional children's picture books, books which reaffirm the value of the 'classic' children's picture book each time they are published (*Outside Over There, Dear Mili*, and so on). Not for Sendak the garish pop-up books of Jan Pienowski or the crayonned sentimentality of Raymond Briggs. Sendak is not interested in street slang, in grappling with serious 'issues' (urban deprivation, racism, classism, sexism, poverty, disease, war), or in being hip and fashionable.

Maurice Sendak sticks to what he knows (and loves) best – the traditional children's picture book, with text in one white space, and the illustration in another. No jumbled text, no trendy typography, no colourful magazine-style layouts, no 'blip publishing' in small boxes, no computer and video simulations or pop promo editing for him. Instead, classic compositions, using Renaissance-inspired roman typefaces (Bembo, Bodoni, Goudy), generous amounts of white space, unfussy layouts, good quality paper, clothbound binding, and large, full-colour illustrations.

I have long loved the illustrations of British artist Tony Ross (b. 1938) (they have been a favourite with my children, too). His books, such as *The Treasure of Cosy Cove* (1989), revel in the art of children's illustration. Ross's picture books are marked by a quirky, humorous tone (as in *I Want My Potty, I Want My Dinner, The Boy Who Cried Wolf* and *The Three Pigs*). Ross has tackled fairy tales, such as *Little Red Riding Hood*. His version of *Hansel and Gretel*, in bright watercolours, seems to use Maurice Sendak's influence. Ross's witch, for instance, appears very similar to Sendak's bulbous-nosed witch in Sendak's own illustration for *Hansel and Gretel* in *The Juniper Tree.*

Maurice Sendak's influence turns up in all manner of places. Children's illustrators continually acknowledge his influence: sometimes in overt ways, sometimes secretly. *The Monster Bed* (1988) by Jeanne Willis, is a Sendakian tale, told, unusually, from the monsters', not the humans', point-of-view (a sequel, *The Monster Storm*, appeared in 1995). The story tells of dinosaur-type monster, Dennis, who is scared of humans under his bed, reversing the usual scenario of children's stories, of children being frightened by monsters under their beds (Pixar/ Disney used the idea in their 2001 film *Monsters, Inc*).[4] It is the illustrations, though, that are clearly derived in part from Sendak's work. The illustrator,

Susan Varley, even gives a statement on the imprint page saying

> *The artist gratefully acknowledges the permission granted by Maurice Sendak for the use of characters from* Where the Wild Things Are, *© 1963 by Maurice Sendak.*

Sendakian motifs appear in the first picture of the story: a Sendakian dog sits next to a picnicing man. The child monster, Dennis, has cuddly toys that are based on the monsters in *Where the Wild Things Are*. There are drawings on the wall like Max's in *Wild Things*.

The lighter, earlier Maurice Sendak (of *Kenny's Window* and *The Moon Jumpers*) is reflected in children's book illustrators such as Gyo Fujikawa (in her *The Night Before Christmas* and *A Child's Garden of Verses*); Hans Fischer (in *The Good-for-Nothings*) has some of the lightness of touch of Sendak's art, that free-flowing line which Sendak could use a lot more; William DuBois has created flying sequences that recall Sendak (as in *Lion*), as have Marcia Brown (in *The Wild Swans*), Reiner Zimnik (the airborne boy in *Bills Ballonfahrt*), and Bill Sokol (in the very Sendakian *A Child's Book of Dreams*); Irene Haas' children recall Sendak's early work (in *A Little House of Your Own*, 1954), as do Margaret Bloy Graham's children (in *The Plant Sitter*) and Janosch's (Horst Eckert) (in *Schuddelbuddel sagt Gutnacht*).

Children's book illustrators who have used dense pen-and-ink line drawings recalling Maurice Sendak's art include Erik Blegvad, whose *Flivver, the Heroic Horse* (by Lee Kingman) has an open, relaxed feel; Leonard Weisgard's *The Secret River* evokes the tender scenes of childhood that Sendak evoked in *The Moon Jumpers, The Nutshell Library* and *Higglety Pigglety Pop!* Some of F.K. Waechter's work looks Sendakian: the Sendak spirit is alive in the densely cross-hatched pen-and-ink drawings filled in with soft watercolours (in *Die Bauern im Brunnen*, 1978); Tomi Ungerer's children's illustrations similarly go for a 19th century, European atmosphere (as in *Das grosse liederbuch*, 1975). Ungerer (b. 1931) is a friend of Sendak's.

More in tune with Maurice Sendak's mischievous approach to children's fiction is Roald Dahl (1917-90), whose books feature naughty, anarchic and independent kids which fitted the social changes of the 1960s and 1970s. Sendak was never as vicious as Dahl – old women were never called 'hags' in Sendak's books. The sparky behaviour of Dahl's children is more in tune with Sendak's own heroes and heroines than characters from Beatrix Potter or A.A. Milne. The Ahlbergs' books (Janet and Allan) have also become classics, from their first joint work, *The Brick Street Boys*, to 1993's *It Was a Dark and Stormy Night*.[6] In the Ahlbergs' books the texts and pictures meld in a Sendakian way. The Ahlbergs also cared greatly for fable and fairy tale, which is central to Sendak's art.

British illustrators such as Brian Wildsmith, Raymond Briggs, John Burningham and Reg Cartwright are variously celebrated, but Maurice Sendak seems more valuable, and more important, finally. Raymond Briggs' books are made up like comicbooks, with their pages formatted like cartoon strips, which makes them well-suited to animation. Briggs (b. 1934) has achieved a certain kind of fame, his books *Where the Wind Blows, The Snowman* and *Father Christmas* have been made into animated films. *The Snowman* and *Father Christmas* are broadcast on TV every Christmas.

A pity, really, that Maurice Sendak doesn't have the same kind of annual Christmas outing (like Dr Seuss's *Grinch* cartoon). It would be great to see *Where the Wild Things Are* or *Outside Over There* in a deluxe animation, meticulously reproducing the look of Sendak's luminous illustrations. If one of Sendak's trilogy (*Where the Wild Things Are, In the Night Kitchen* and *Outside Over There*) were made into an animated film, however, more detail and incident would need to be added (this happened with the 1980s opera and the 2009 live-action adaption of *Where the Wild Things Are*).

And finally: Dr Seuss, the only serious competitor with

Maurice Sendak for the title of the Great Children's Book Illustrator of recent times. No one in modern children's book illustration matches Dr Seuss (Theodor Geisel, 1904-91) for sheer anarchy and exuberance. Not even Jan Pienowski at his most pop-up crazy (in *Haunted House*, 1979, for example) can equal the zaniness of Dr Seuss. In *The Cat In the Hat, How the Grinch Stole Christmas, Horton Hatches the Egg*, and other books, Dr Seuss produced wild cartoon characters whose knockabout antics recall the Marx Brothers, the Three Stooges and the golden age of silent film comedy.

Just as important as the grinning creatures of Dr Seuss was the rhyming text which had a driving power all of its own. As poetry it was crude, but as prose for a children's book, it was irresistible (*The Cat In the Hat* contained just 237 words). Seuss's books expressed in fantastic and exaggerated language and imagery basic conflicts and anxieties in people. In *The Cat In the Hat* (1957) the tensions are between the wild, mischievous side, and the controlling, sane side, as the Cat usurps the boredom and normality of the children's afternoon, while the exasperated fish begs him to stop his antics, as Mother will return home soon. Yet the Cat in the Hat clears up the mess he's made. He shows how there is a place for wildness and free expression, and shows how it can be reined in again, afterwards. *The Cat in the Heat*, improbable and delicious though it is, is a modern-day fairy tale, which brings the wildness of the outside world into the house.[5] While Max's room in *Where the Wild Things Are* dissolves into a forest, followed by a voyage of a year and a day, the wild zone of the forest erupts inside the children's house in *The Cat In the Hat* and stays there.

IN CONCLUSION

IN THIS BOOK, I have tried to indicate just some of the ways in which Maurice Sendak is a powerful and magical book illustrator. There is always some extra element which one cannot describe precisely. Call it 'mystery', 'magic', whatever. It is that something that Sendak has (but so many others do not have). Few children's book illustrators have the same mastery and insights as Sendak.

There are too many children's books illustrators who produce mediocre work, hack work. Too often, they are ticking over, making a living. Something more is required, and Maurice Sendak provides that. He gives back the magic into children's book illustrations. He recovers the wonder of children's stories and childhood through illustrations that are vigorously and skillfully executed. Sendak re-creates the strangeness and sometimes grotesque quality of 19th century book illustration. He recovers the sense of first seeing Gustave Doré, or John Tenniel's illustrations of *Alice's Adventures in Wonderland*.

Maurice Sendak's illustrations have passed into the mainstream establishment of culture, they have the look of classics such as Arthur Rackham, Walter Crane, Edward Ardizzone, Aubrey Beardsley or Randolph Caldecott. Sendak's illustrations capture that 19th century quality of simultaneous crudity and sophistication, that simultaneous sense of horror and beauty, that simultaneous innocence and knowingness. Sendak recaptures that feeling of how odd it was to see George Cruikshank illustrations – the gawdiness of them, the bawdiness, the vulgarity and the vivid sense of being alive. (Other book illustrators in this shadowy, post-19th century vein include Mervyn Peake, the eccentric and lovable artist who created the eccentric and lovable *Gormenghast* trilogy, and atmospheric, tenebrous illustrations, such as those Doré-like pictures to S.T. Coleridge's *The Rime of the Ancient Mariner*. There is a woodcut and etching/ print tradition, too, among book illustrators in this genre: John Farleigh, for example, with his Eric Gillian etchings, or Gwendolen Raverat, or Harry Clarke's post-Rackham/ Beardsley illustrations, as in his work for Edgar Allen Poe's *Tales of Mystery and Imagination*).

Too many contemporary children's book illustrators produce flat, lifeless work. There is no depth – either spatial or tonal, or psychological. Compare contemporary illustrators to the 18th, 19th and early 20th century illustrators – to the anonymous illustrators in *Tabart's Popular Stories* (1804), *The History of the Yellow Dwarf* (1852), or the marvellous little woodcuts of Thomas Bewick and George Cruikshank, each one a treat. Or compare contemporary illustrations with the richness of illustrations by Walter Crane, Eleanor Vere Boyle, Arthur Rackham *et al*, where every inch of the picture is lovingly covered with marks.

The thinking these days is that children require light, fluffy imagery, full of pastel pinks and yellows, with clearly defined black lines around forms (echoing cel animation on TV), and nothing too difficult or worrying to contemplate. Maurice Sendak shows that it doesn't have to be like that. Sendak took the illustration style of the 19th and early 20th century, a style (in the art of Walter Crane, George Cruikshank, and Gustave Doré) that was intended for consumption by adults, and offered it to children. While nursery rhymes and fairy tales were made by and for adults (in the 18th and 19th centuries), Sendak returned them to children. In doing this, Sendak stands high above most other children's picture book illustrators. Sendak's illustrations are simply so much richer, and deeper, than most other illustrators' work. His art is not fussy or complicated, necessarily; rather, it strikes to the heart of the mystery of things, like Leonardo da Vinci's drawings or Albrecht Dürer's woodcuts. As with Leonardo and Dürer, there is a sense of exploration – and play – in Sendak's *œuvre*.

But this sense of play does not mean that Maurice Sendak

produces banal, fluffy, wispy work. Sendak's most important insight, perhaps, was to realize that children could absorb a much richer (and darker) form of book illustration than what was usually served up for them. While publishers shied away from deep and challenging work, wary about being disturbing, Sendak knew that children – like childhood – have ambiguous and mysterious aspects. It is that region, somewhere between deep night dreams and lighter day dreams, between active, conscious fantasizing and casual daydreaming, that Sendak explores. It is the place of wild things – not only outside, over there – but here, always *in here* (where else could it be?).

Illustrations

Maurice Sendak

1. *The Moon Jumpers*, 1959.
2. *Where the Wild Things Are*, 1963.
3. Stage set design for *Where the Wild Things Are*, 1979.
4. Poster for Warner Bros' adaption of *Where the Wild Things Are,* 2009.
5. *Schoolmaster Whackwell's Wonderful Sons*, 1962.
6. *Hector Protector*, 1965.
7. *Lullabies and Night Songs*, 1965.
8. *Zlateh the Goat and Other Stories*, 1966.
9. *Higglety Pigglety Pop!*, 1967.
10. *In the Night Kitchen*, 1970.
11. *The Juniper Tree*, 1973.
12. *Fly By Night*, 1977.
13. *King Grisly-Beard*, 1973
14. *Outside Over There*, 1981, including a sketch.
15. *Nutcracker*, 1984.
16. *Dear Mili*, 1988.

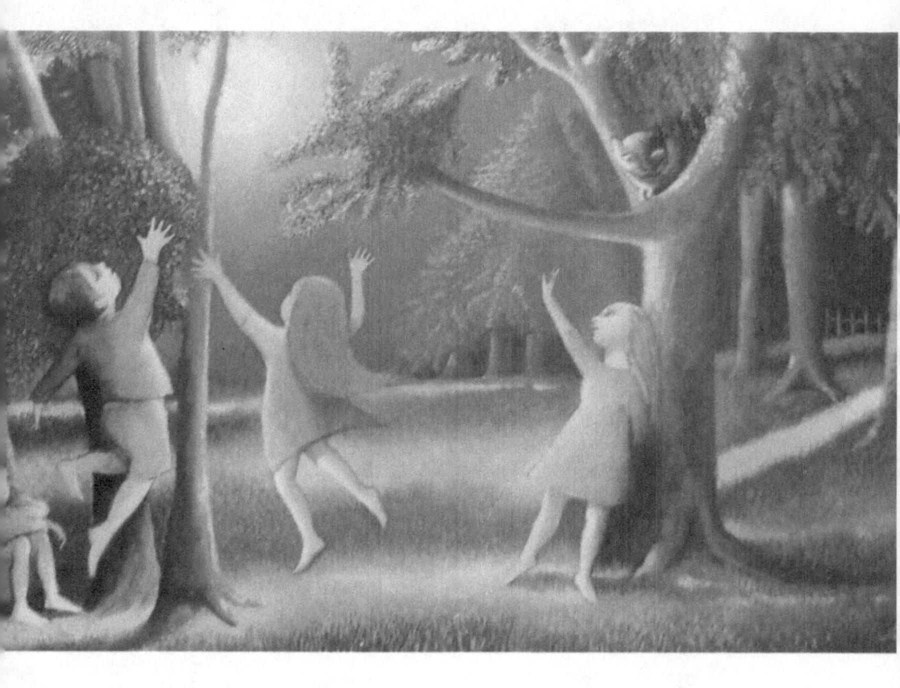

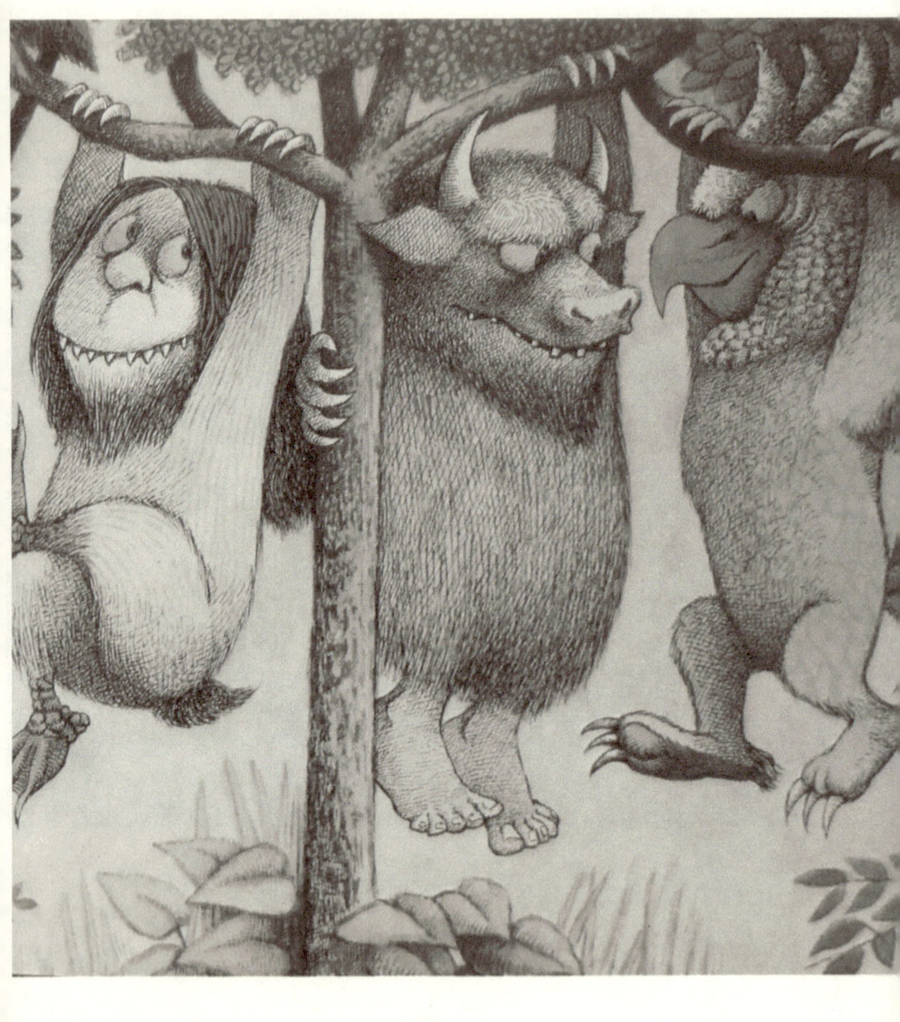

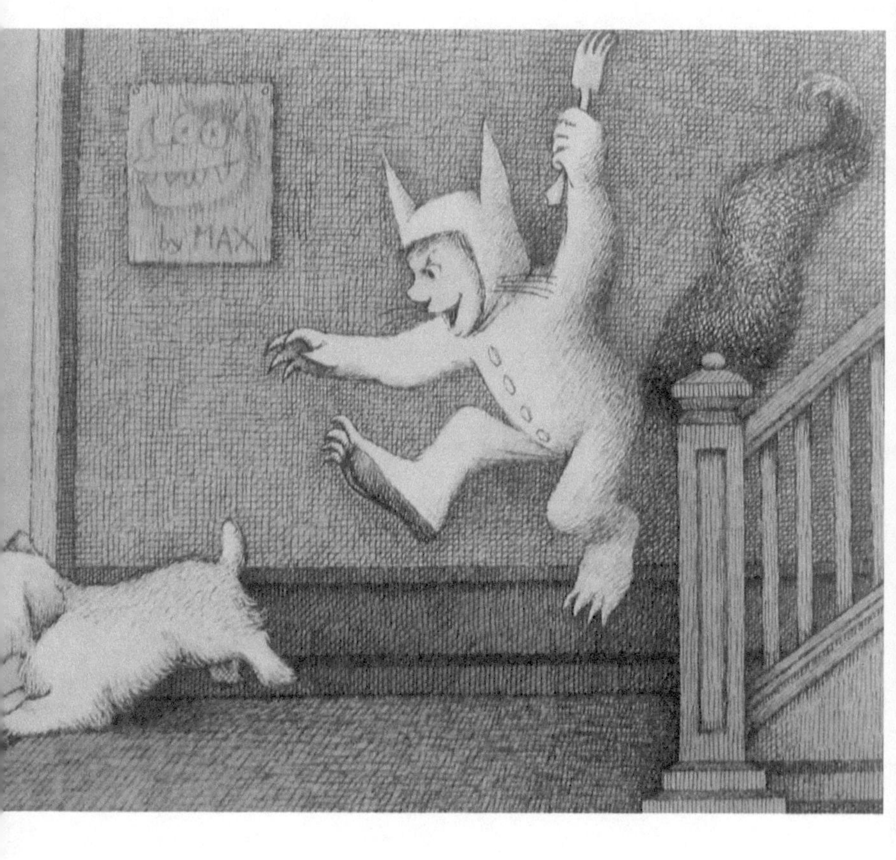
by MAX

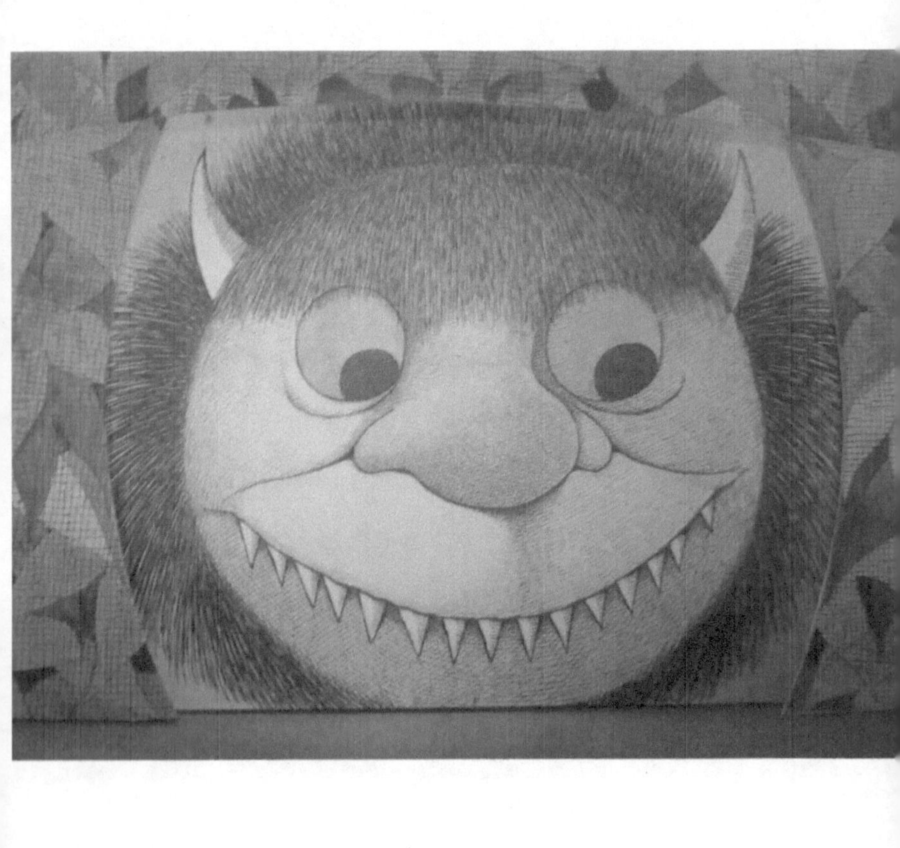

There's one in all of us.

WHERE THE WILD THINGS ARE

Fall 2009

LEGENDARY

www.wherethewildthingsare.com

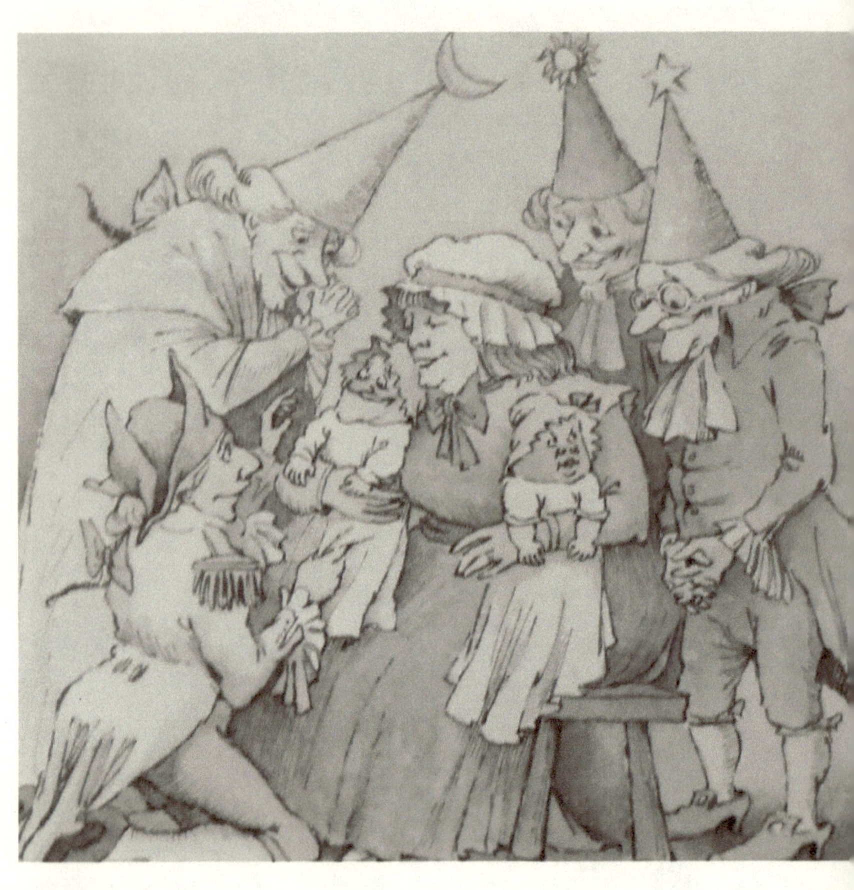

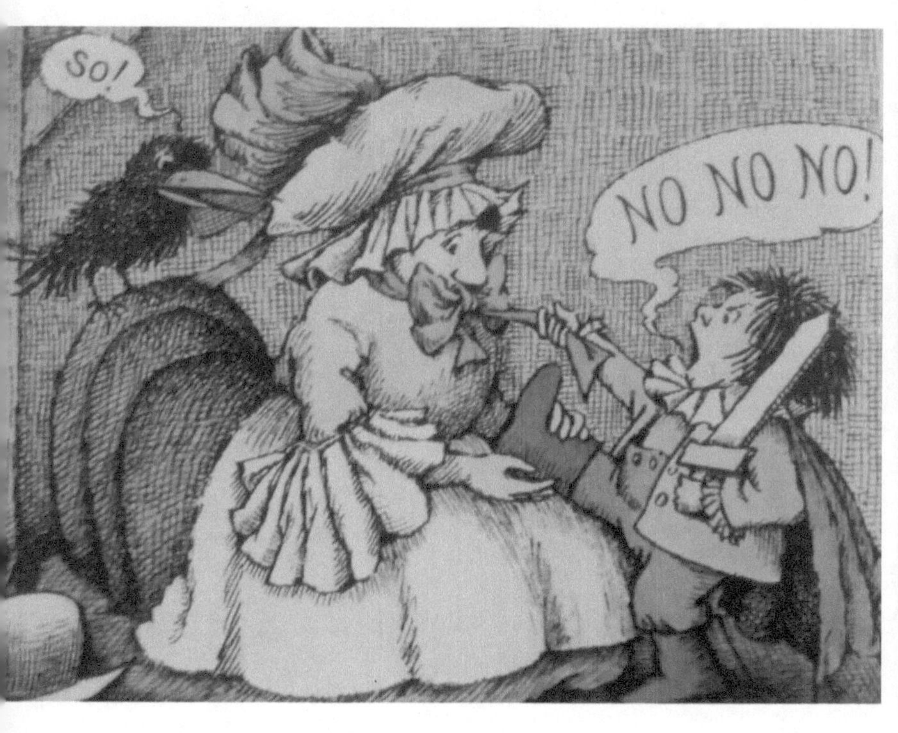
So!
NO NO NO!

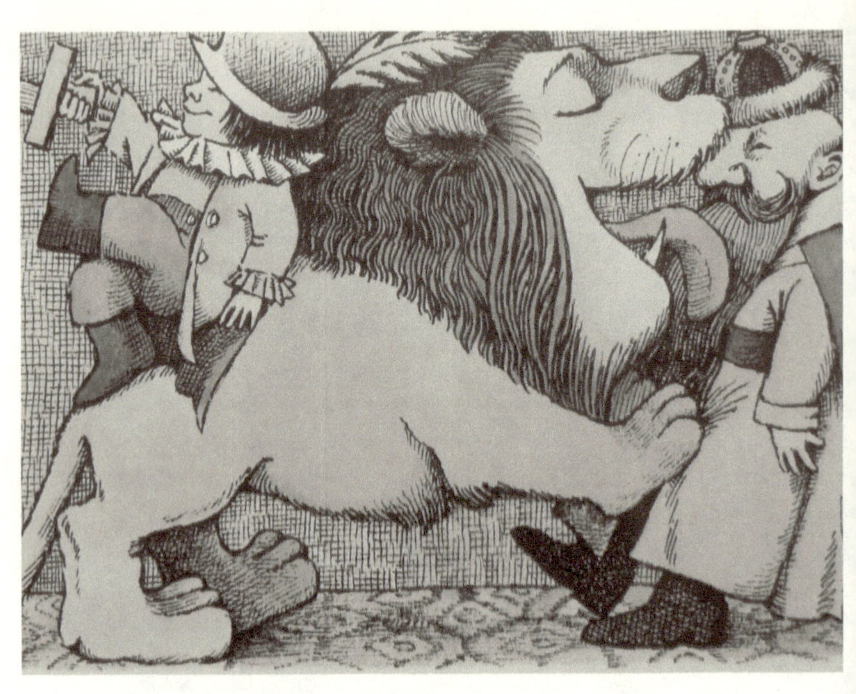

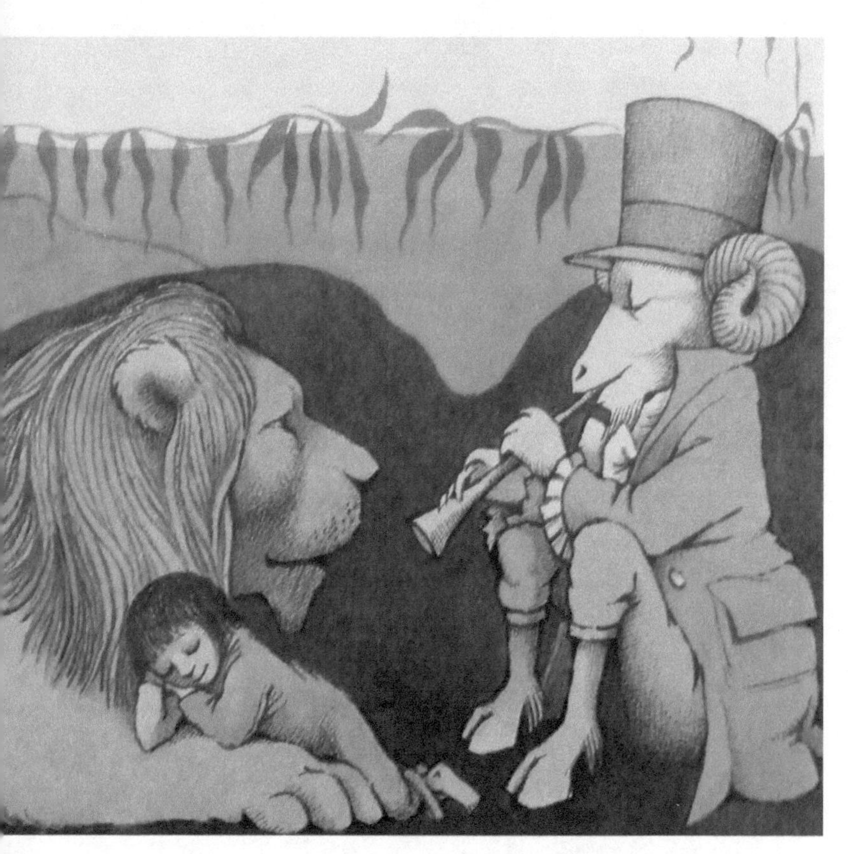

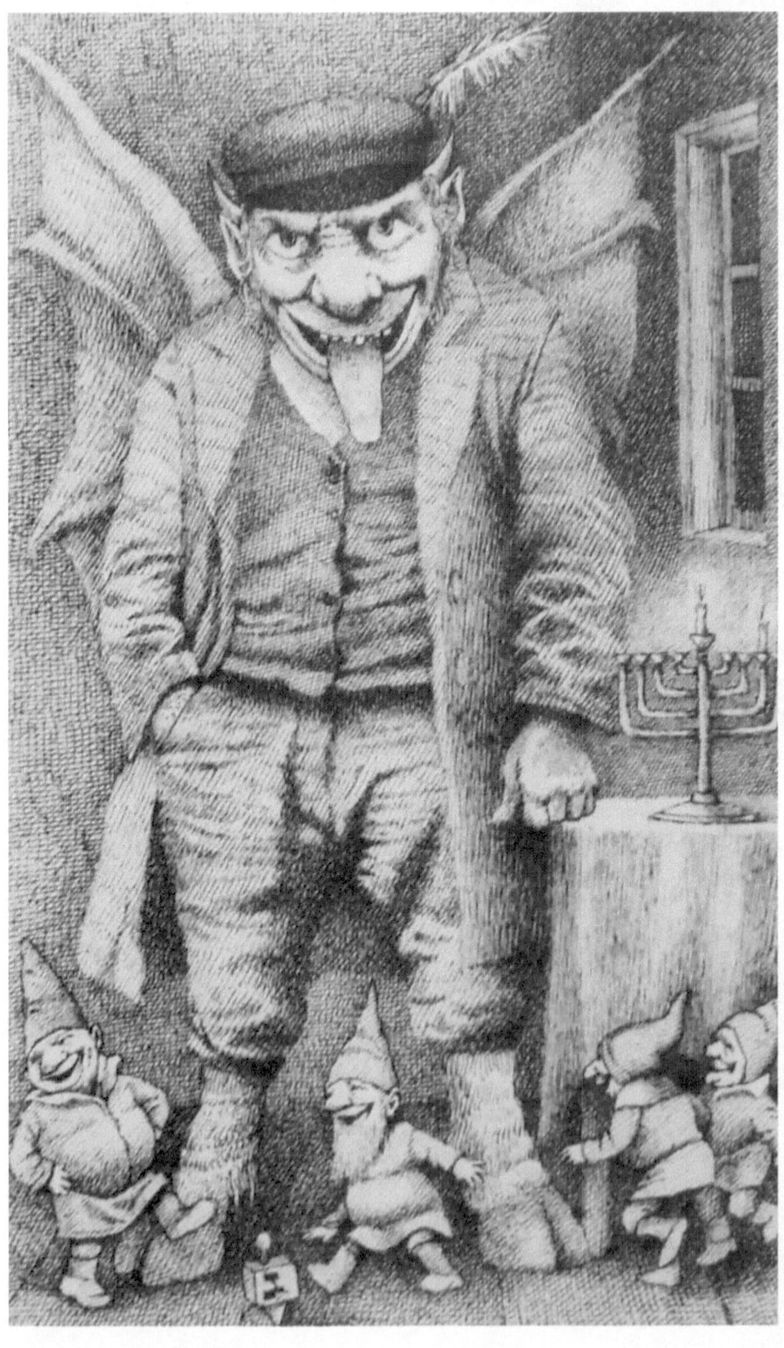

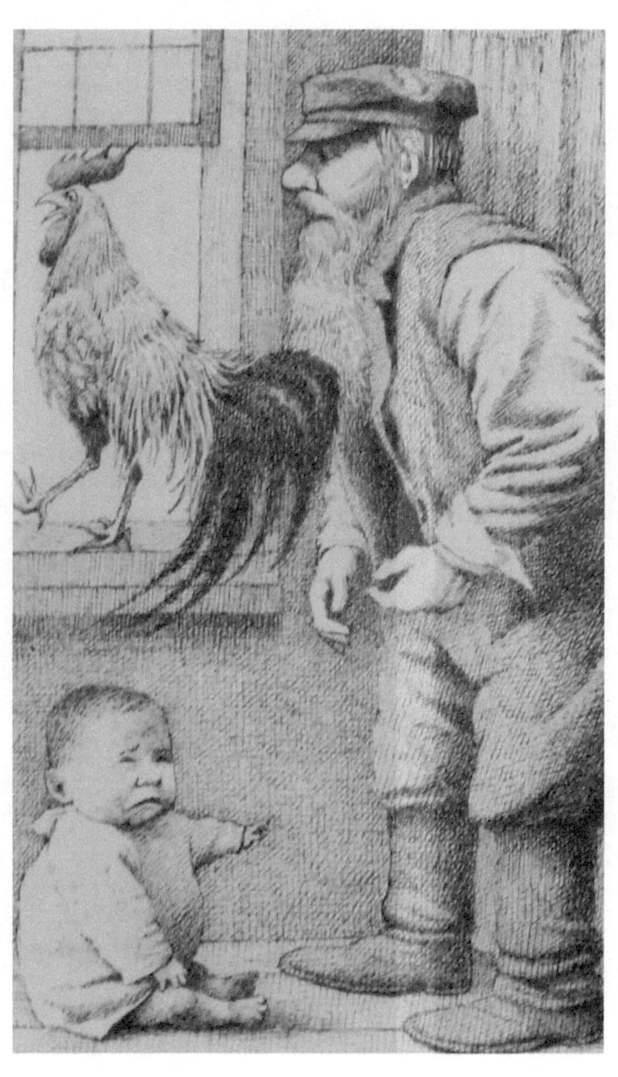

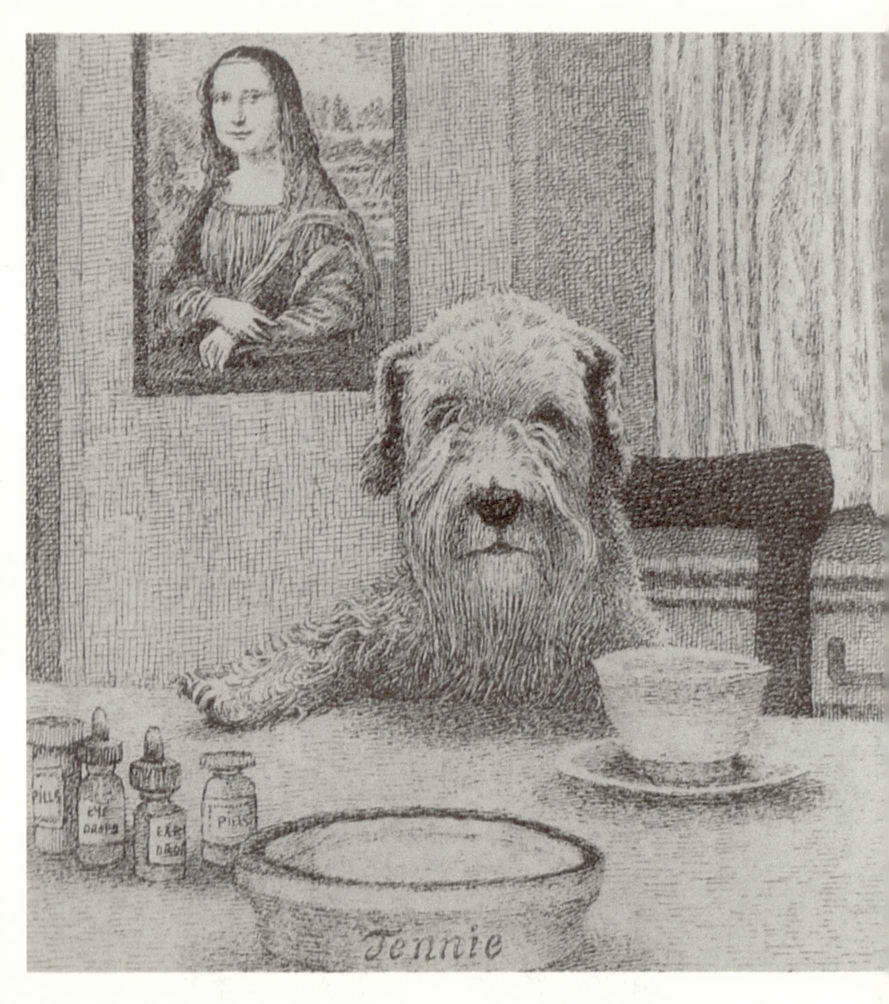
PILLS
EYE DROPS
PILLS
Jennie

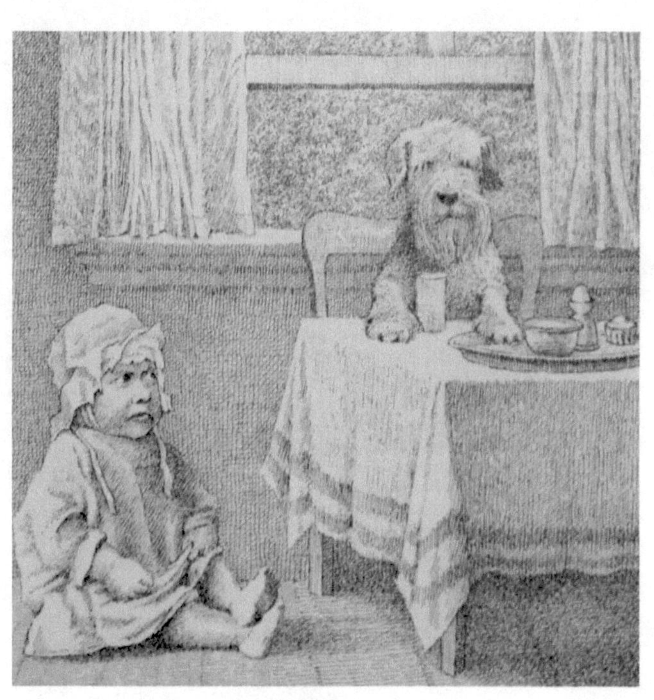

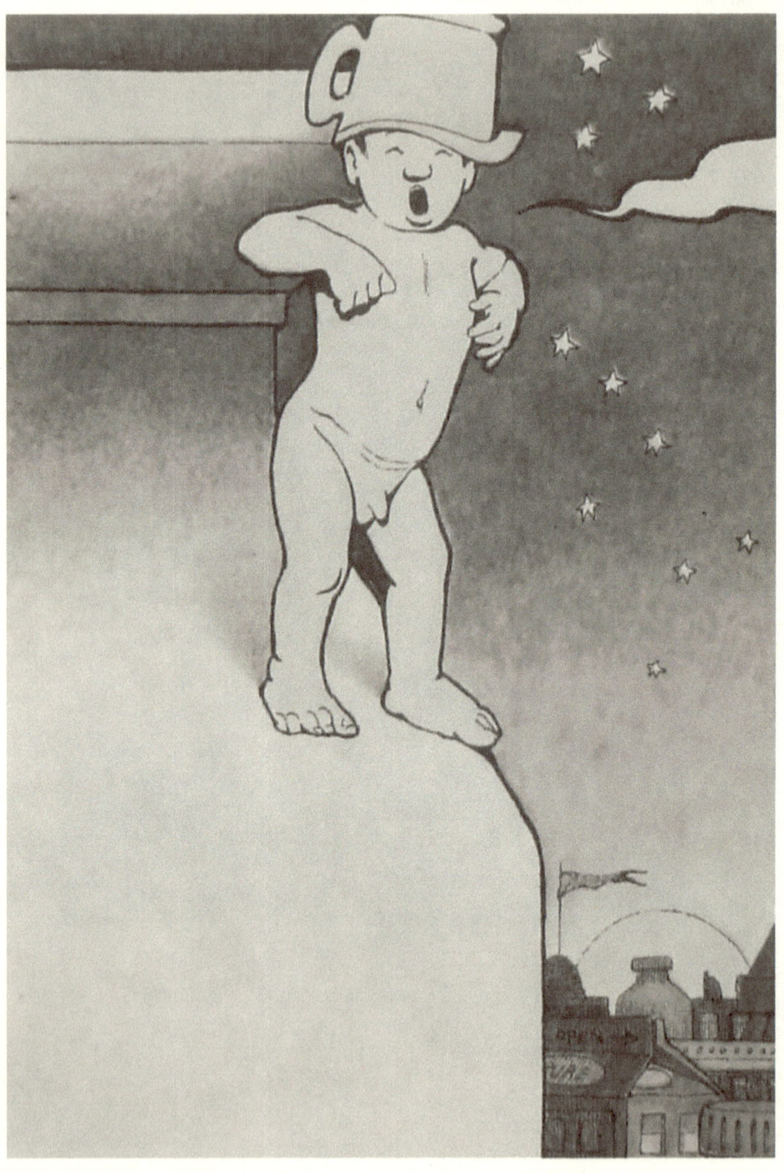

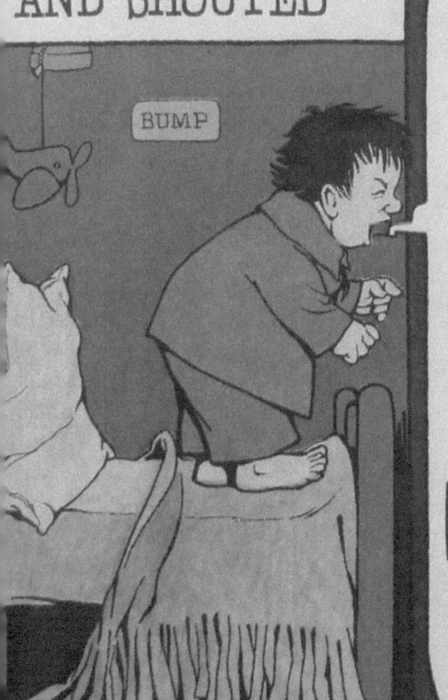

QUIET DOWN THERE!

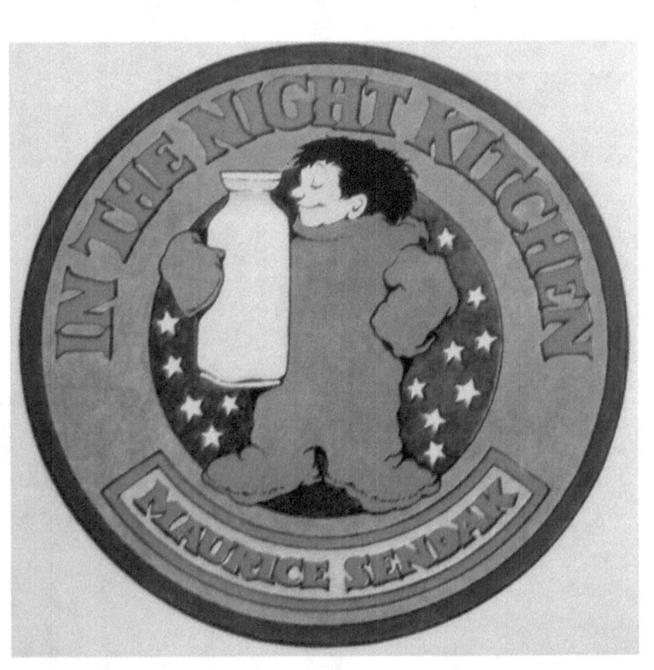
IN THE NIGHT KITCHEN
MAURICE SENDAK

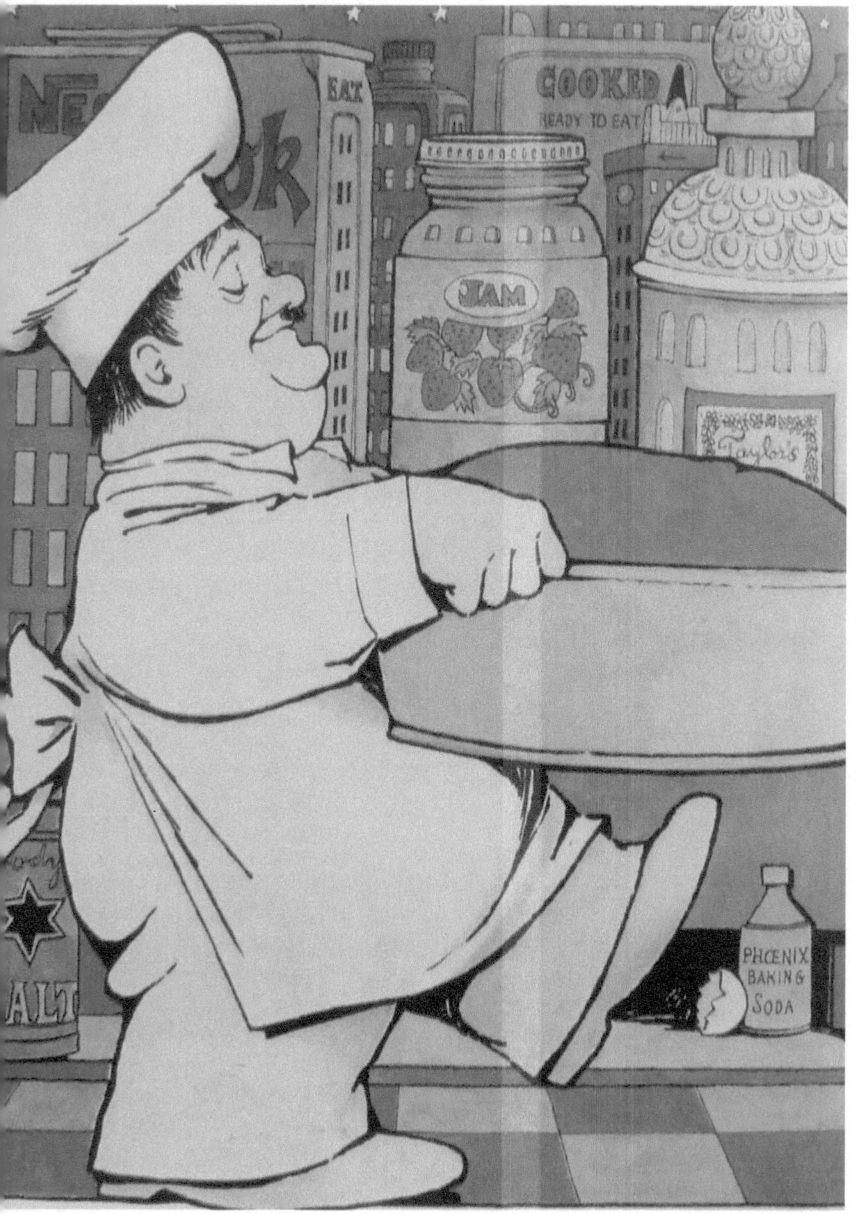
EAT
COOKED
READY TO EAT
JAM
Taylor's
PHŒNIX
BAKING
SODA

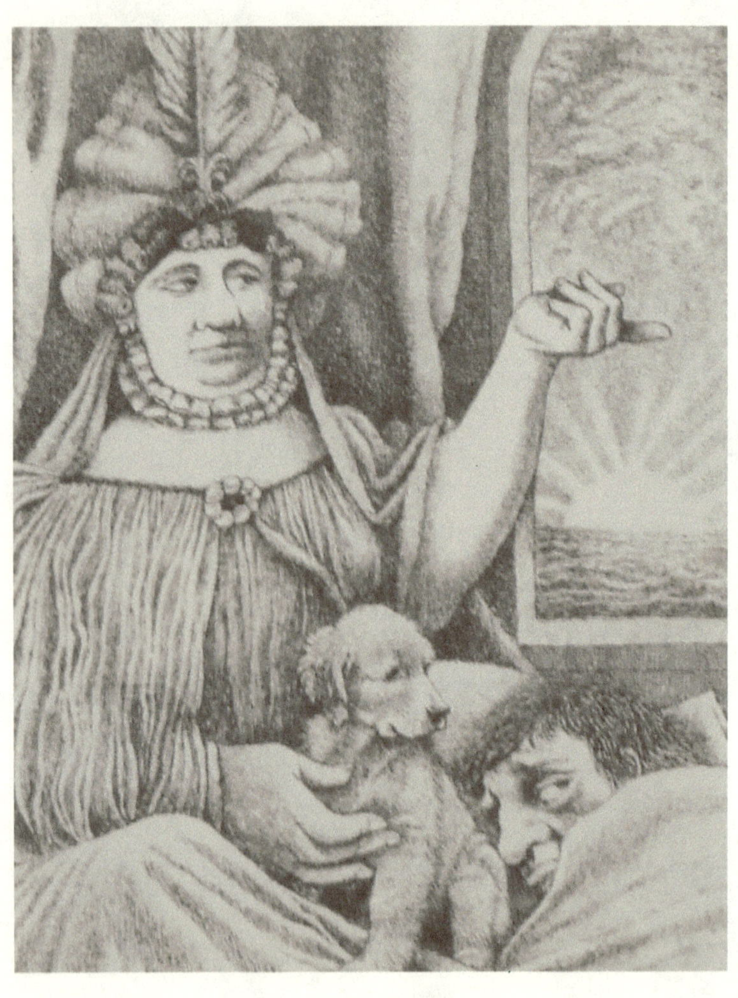

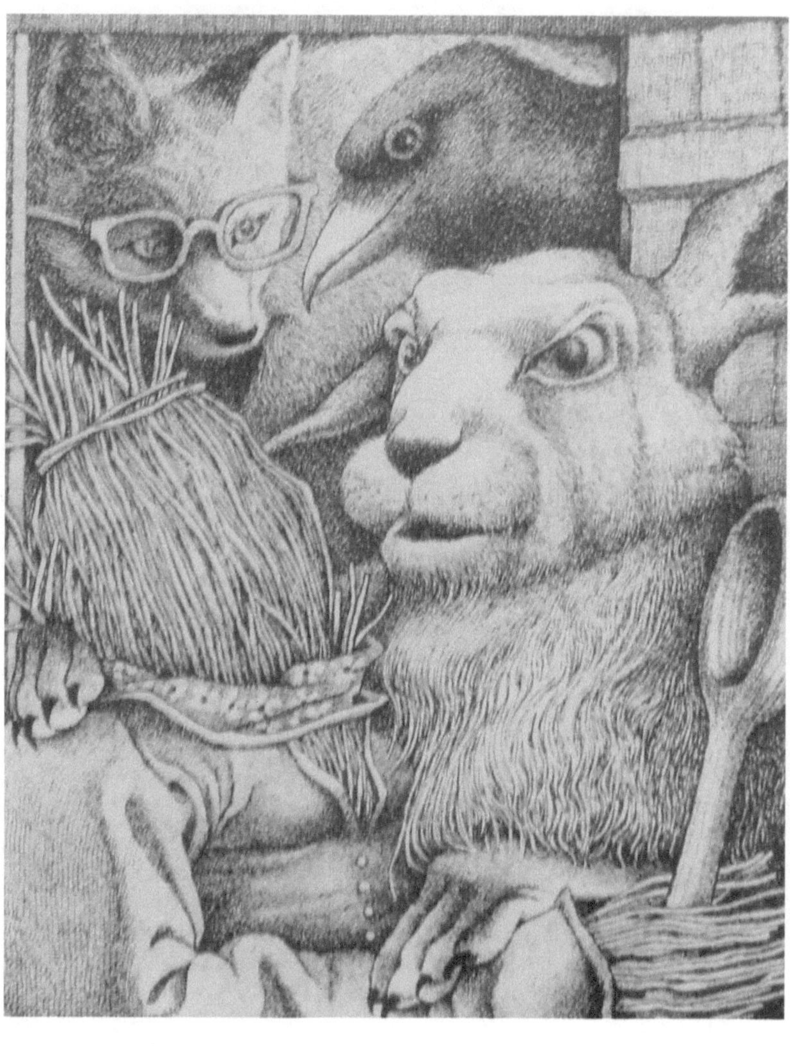

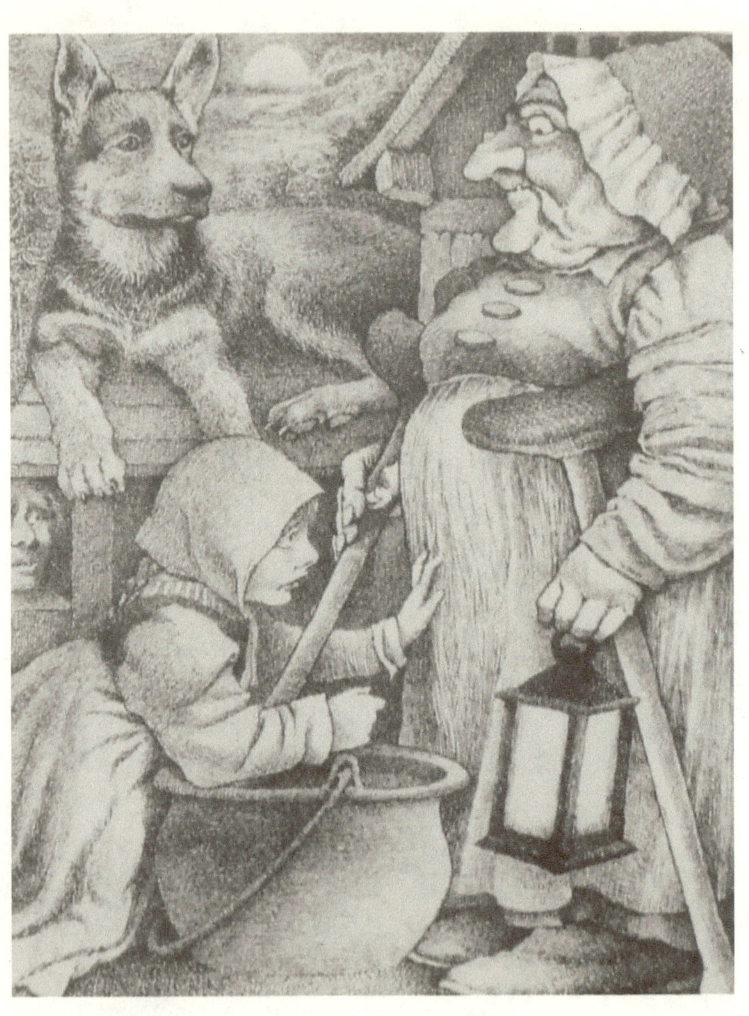

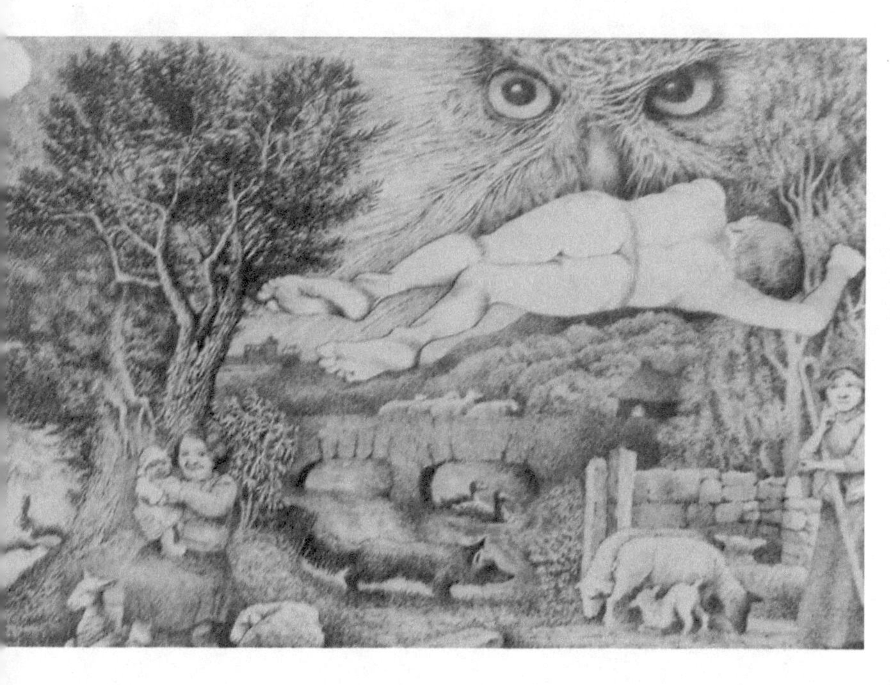

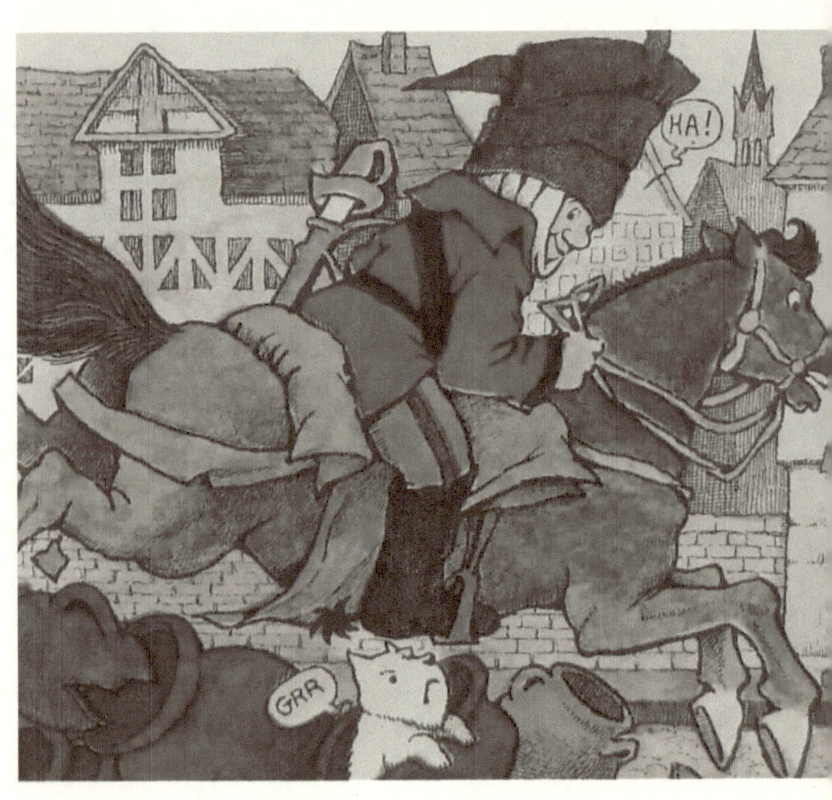
HA!
GRR

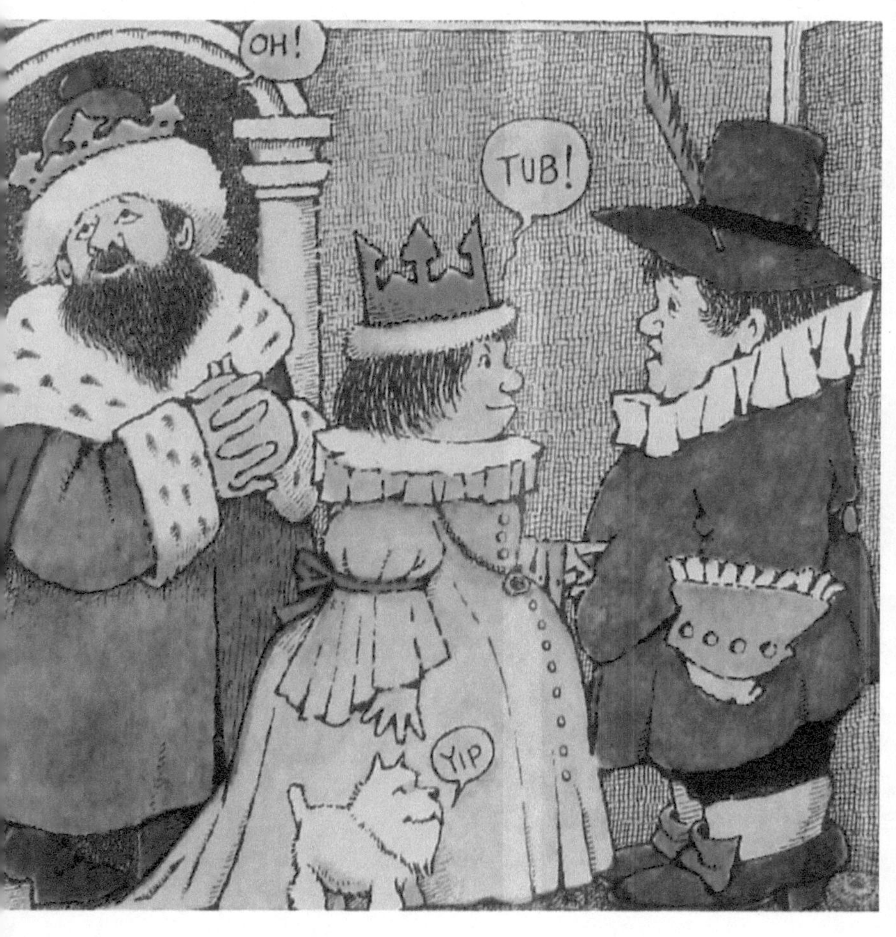
OH!
TUB!
YIP

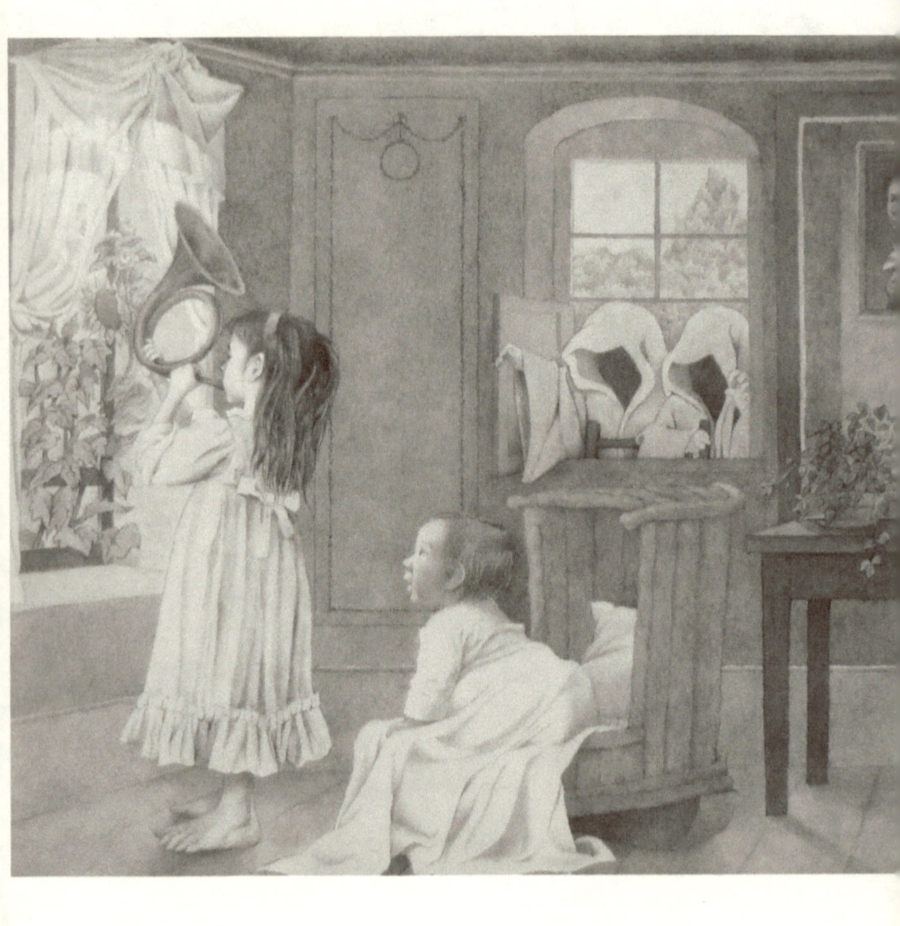

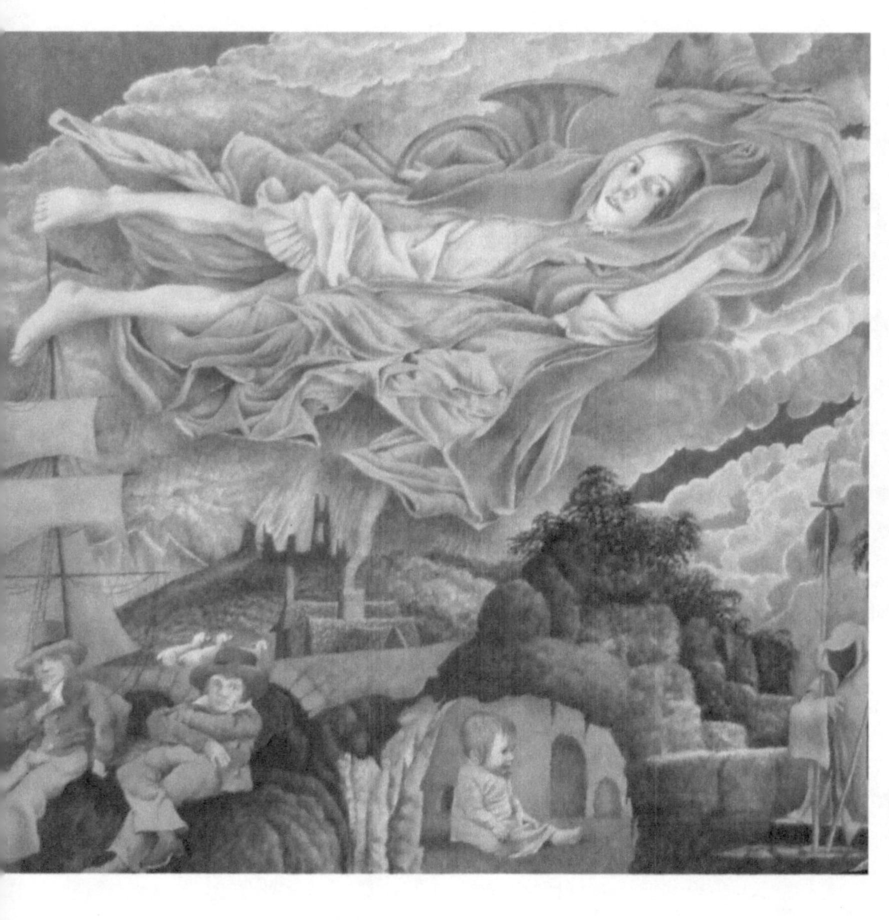

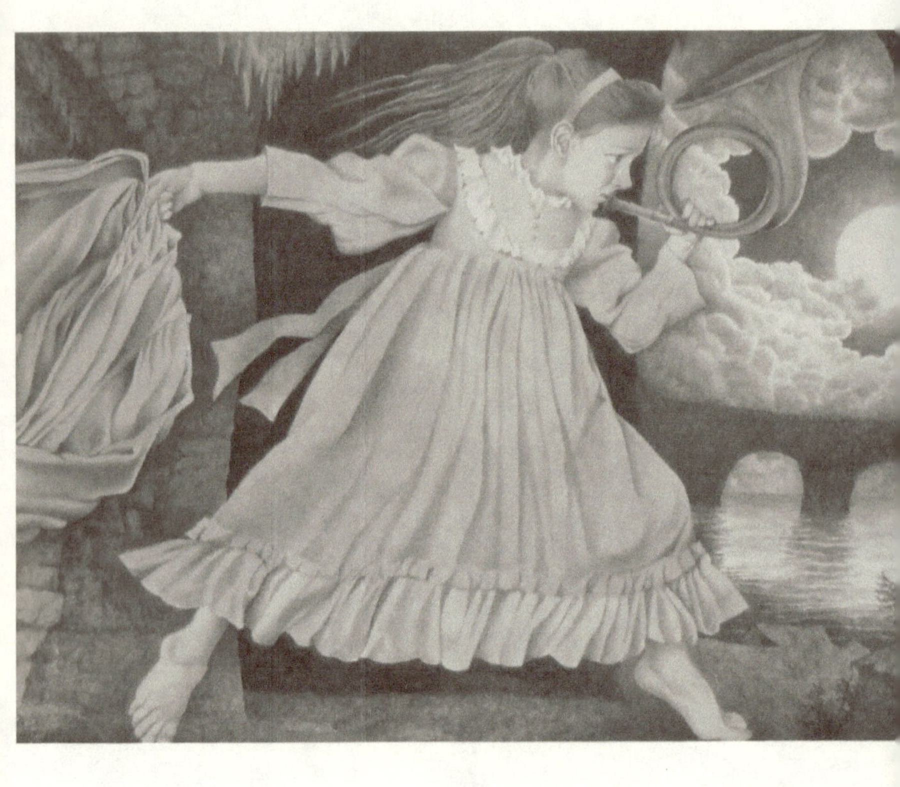

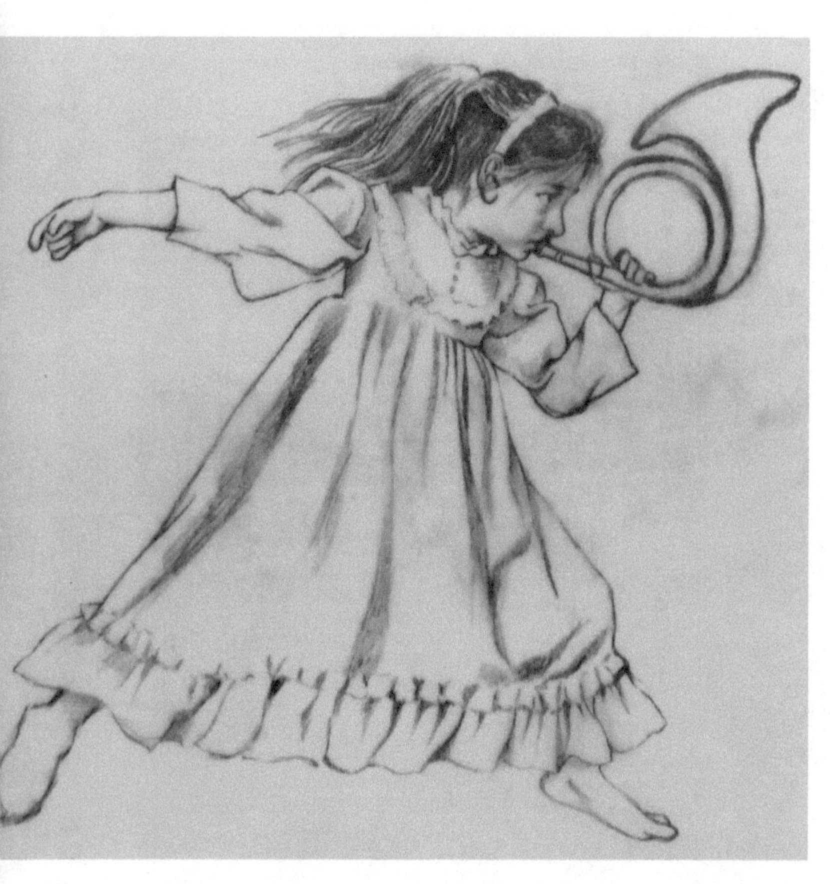

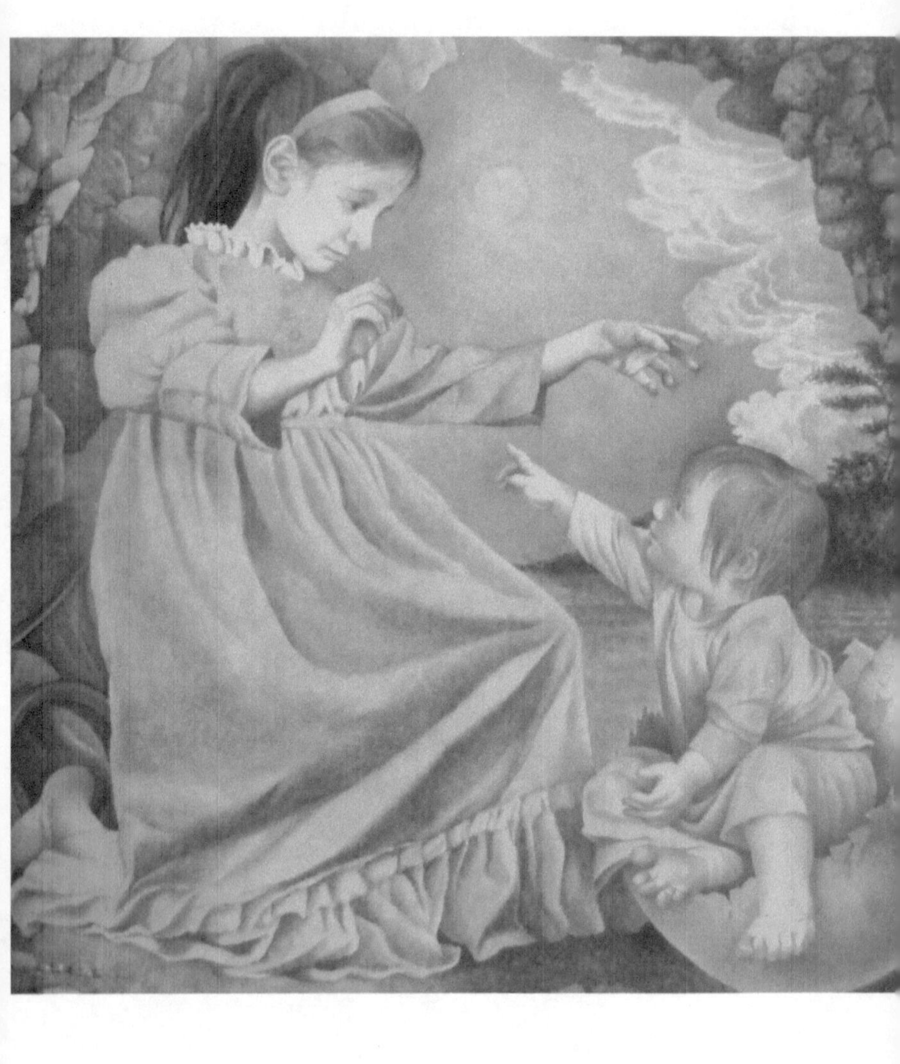

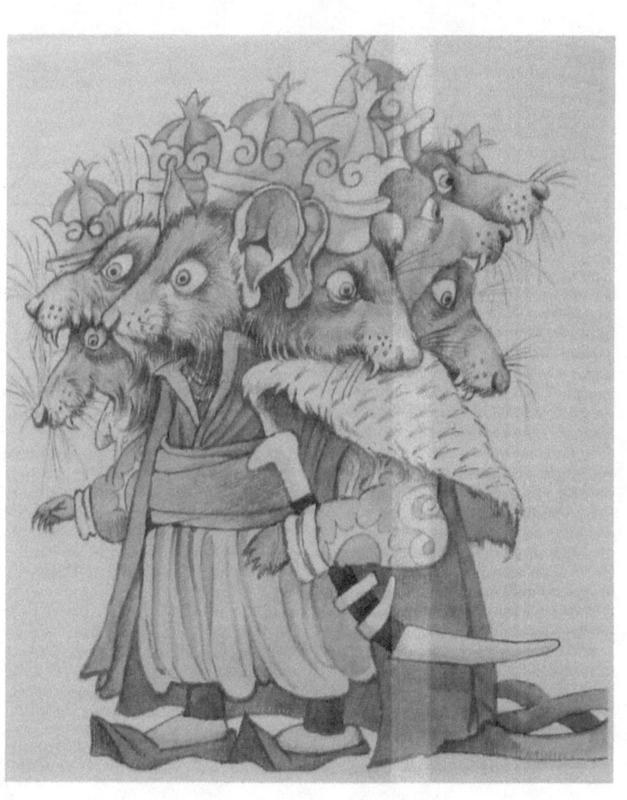

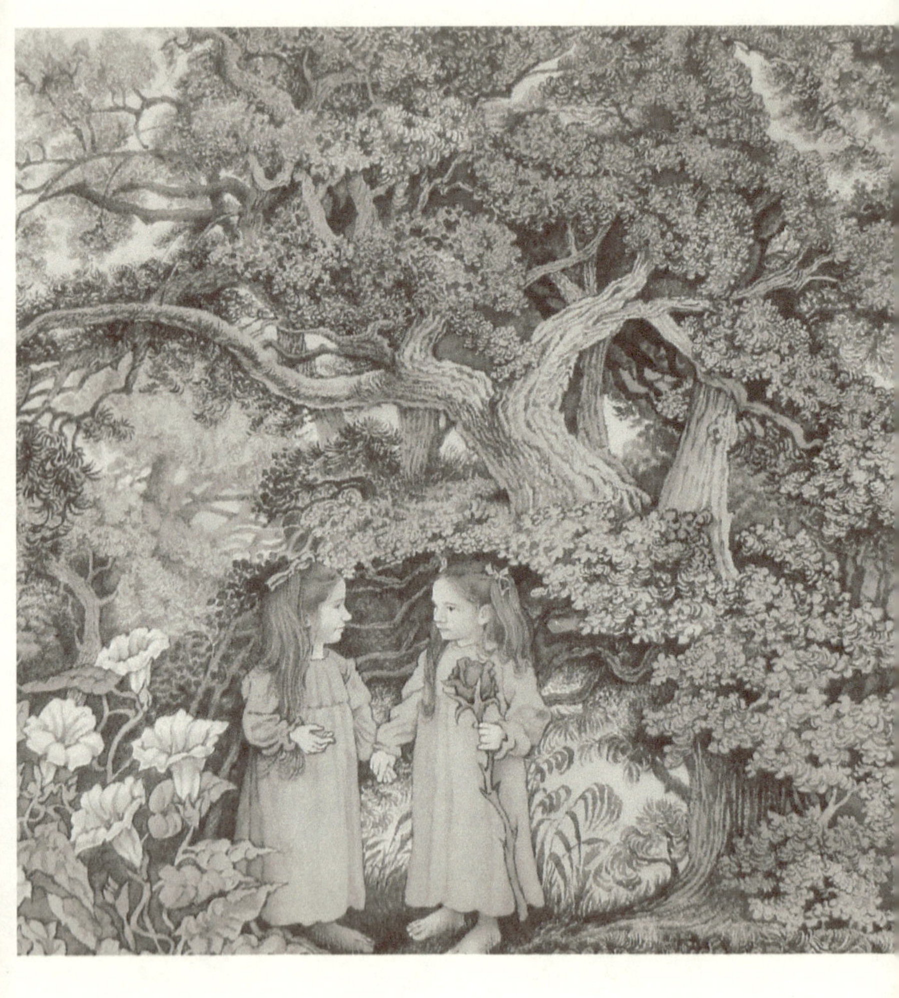

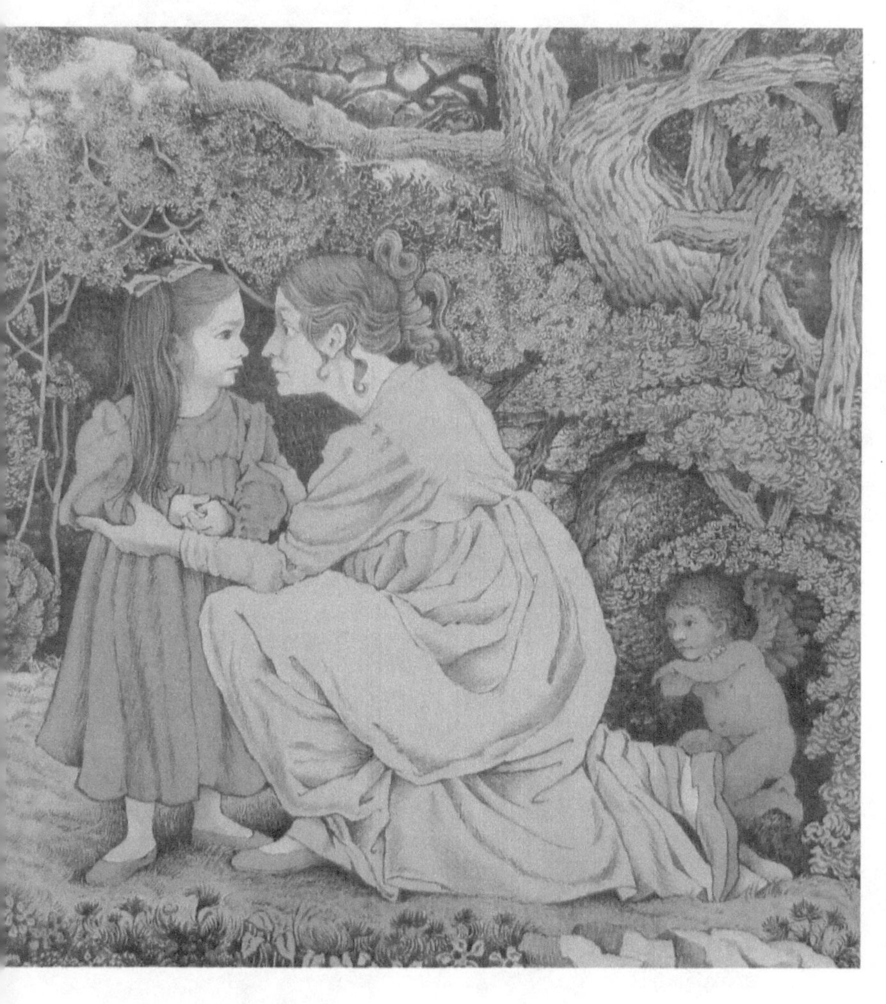

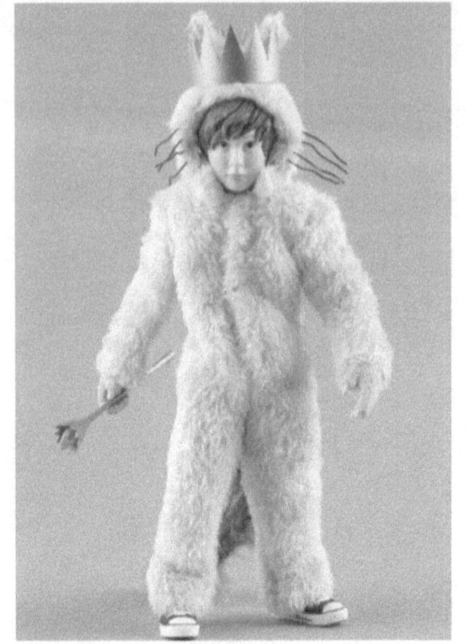

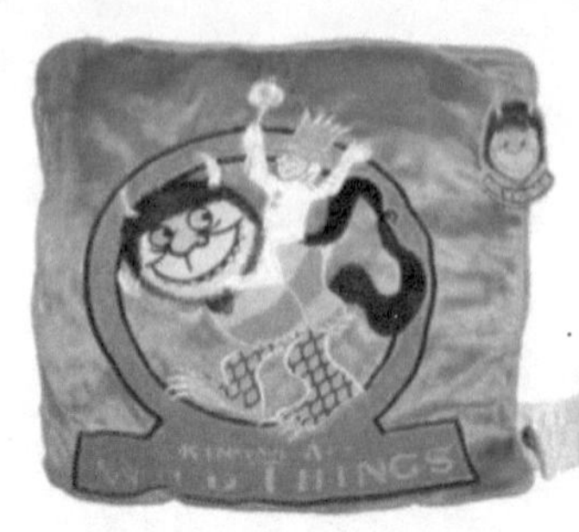

Maurice Sendak's
REALLY ROSIE starring the Nutsh
MUSIC BY CAROLE KING

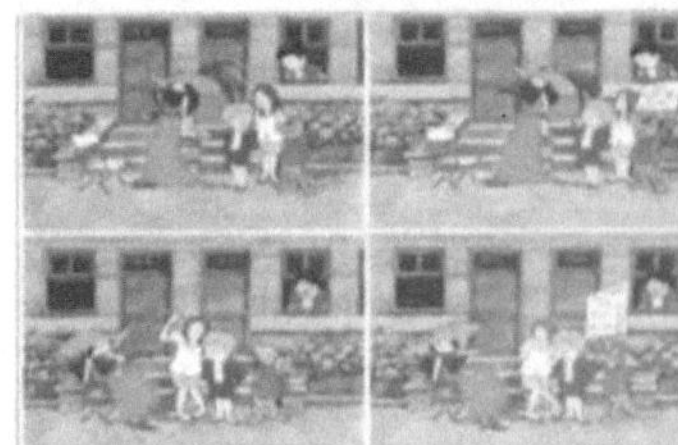

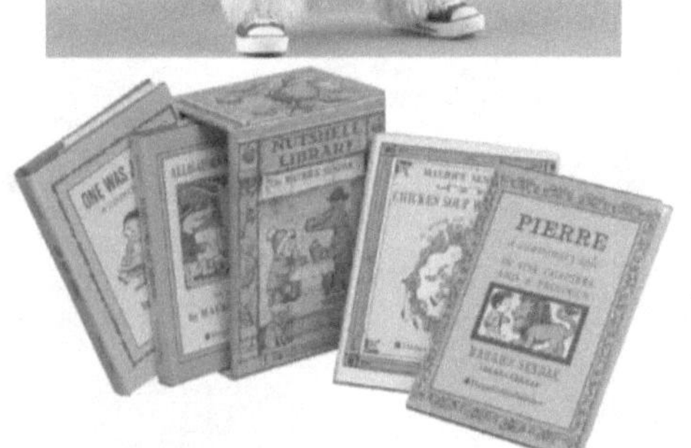

Some merchandize based on Maurice Sendak's books

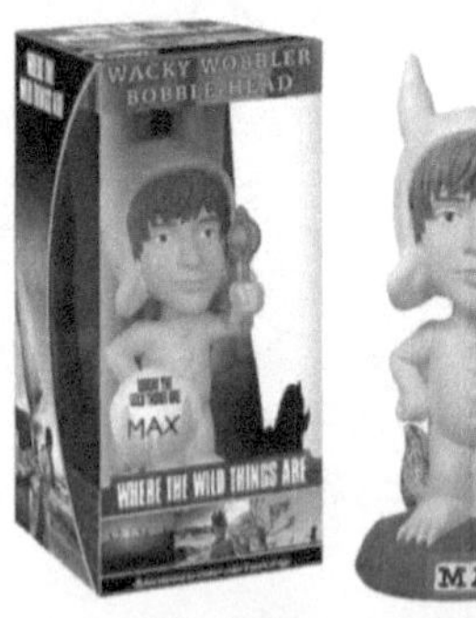

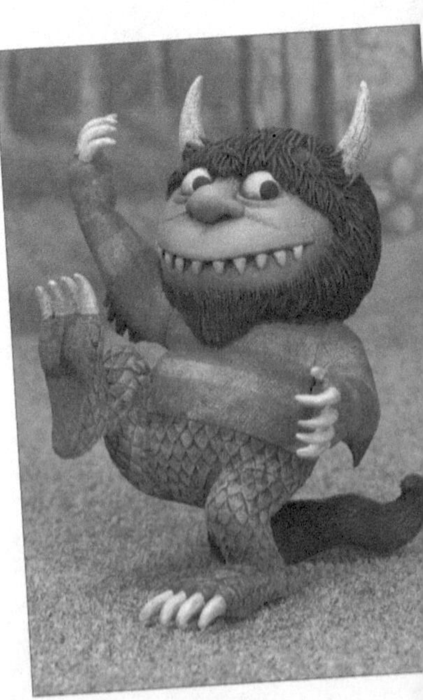

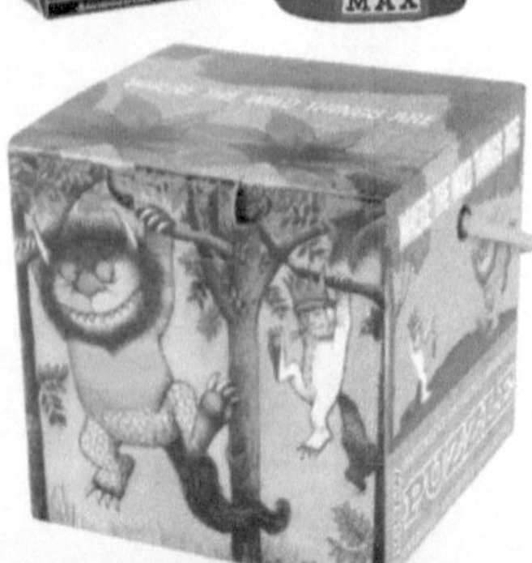

Notes

I Introductory

1. M. Sendak: "Walt Disney", *TV Guide*, Nov 11, 1978, in C, 107.
2. U. Nordstrom, quoted in B. Bader, 1976, 427.
3. Joyce Whalley and Tessa Chester write in *A History of Children's Book Illumination* of Maurice Sendak's trilogy and its theme of how 'children master their various negative feelings (anger, guilt, fear, boredom)', creating an 'entirely new concept in picture books for young children and one that was to provoke a good deal of controversy.' (218-9).
4. 'Kiddiebookland is where we live. Didn't you know? It's next to Neverneverville and Peterpanburg.' (M. Sendak, "A Conversation with Walter Lorraine", C, 191).
5. In H. Carpenter, 1999, 476-7.
6. Elaine Showalter, ed. *The New Feminist Criticism,* Virago, 1986

II Children's Book Illustration

1. In the last image of *Where the Wild Thing Are*, for example, Maurice Sendak alludes to *Adam* by Auguste Rodin, where Max has his hand on his forehead. (W. Moebius, 1986, in P. Hunt, 1990, 138).
2. T. Shippey, 1982, 6.
3. N. Mikkelsen writes:

   it is probably safe to say that for most preschool children, *the* central issue is going to be some variant of the relationship between themselves (as small, vulnerable people) and a parent or parent-figure (perceived as a large, powerful person who may be either loving or rejecting, or, most usually, both). (1984)

III Fairy Tales

1. J. Zipes, 2000, xxvi.
2. J. Zipes, 2000, xx.

3. J. Zipes, 1988, 22.
4. See C. Bühler: *Das Märchen und die Phantasie des Kindes*, Springer, Berlin, 1977; Géza Roheim: "Psycho-analysis and the Folk-Tale", *International Journal of Psychoanalysis*, 3, 1922; C.G. Jung: "The Phenomen-ology of the Spirit in Fairy Tales", *Psyche and Symbol*, Anchor, New York, NY, 1958; A. Jaffé: *Bilder und Symbole aus E.T.A. Hoffmanns Märchen "Der goldene Topf"*, Gerstenberg, Zurich, 1978; J. Campbell; M.-L. von Franz; B. Bettelheim; E Fromm, 1957; J. Heuscher, 1963; A. Favat: *The Origins of Interest*, National Council of Teachers of English, Urbana, 1977; V. Propp; M. Lüthi; D. Richter & J. Merkel: *Märchen, Phantasie und Soziales Lernen*, Basis, Berlin, 1974; C. Bürger: "Die soziale Funktion volkstümlicher Erzähl-formen – Sage und Märchen", in H. Ide, 1971; B. Wollenberg: "Märchen und Sprichwort", in H. Ide, 1974; C. Steedman, 1985; R. Sale, 1978.
5. J. Zipes, *The Trials and Tribulations of Little Red Riding Hood*, 46; M. Foucault: *The History of Sexuality*, Pantheon, New York, NY, 1978, 135-9.
6. There is usually a central plot-line or 'spine' to a fairy tale, some central events that cannot be changed without changing the nature of the whole tale. For example, Snow White must eat the poison apple. Before and after that she might do another month of housework, by the fire singing, or the reader may hear nothing of her until the next important event, the dwarves returning home to find her apparently dead. It is, in fact, this moment that Maurice Sendak chose to illustrate in *The Juniper Tree*: the moment when Snow White bites the apple and lies dead; the dwarf looks disturbed; the Queen is shown in triumph, her mirror reflects the poisoned apple.
7. C.G. Jung: *Collected Works*, vol. 4, Rasch, Zurich 1971, 237; see B. Bettelheim, 1976; L. Burns, 1972.
8. There are affinities, though, between *Little Red Riding Hood*, especially in Jack Zipes' interpretation, and Maurice Sendak's illustrations for *Mr Rabbit and the Lovely Present*, where Zipes' explication of the gazes exchanged between Little Red Riding Hood and the wolf echo those of the girl and the rabbit in the title page of *Mr Rabbit*. (P. Nodelman, 1988, 118)
9. 'Like all good art, like our imaginations, the tales repre-sent a sort of incantation by which that wonder is returned to us and by which the half-glimpsed images of that something are called forth', Joyce Thomas, wrote in *Inside the Wolf's Belly: Aspects of the Fairy Tale* (284).
10. Angela Carter writes in *The Virago Book of Fairy Tales:*

The excision of references to sexual and excremental functions, the toning down of sexual situations and the reluctance to include 'indelicate' material – that is, dirty jokes – helped to denaturize the fairy tale and indeed, helped to denature its vision of everyday life. (xvii)

IV *Sendak and Grimm: The Juniper Tree*

1. M. Sendak: "Hans Christian Andersen", *Book Week, The Sunday Herald Tribune*, March 13, 1966.
2. Alison Lurie writes:

   The same fantastical and haunting quality appears in the illustrations to *The Juniper Tree*. Like all Maurice Sendak's work, they are superb. But they come from a darker and stranger side of his genius than the pictures in *In the Night Kitchen* or *Where the Wild Things Are*. They are visions of another and in some ways realer world than this, a dream – or nightmare – world certainly, but one in which the dream gardens contain actual toads, complete to the last wart. They have beauty too, though it is a beauty that sometimes merges into the terrifying: skeletons appear, corpses, hooded ghosts, and a devil that makes the Wild Things look like stuffed toys. (A. Lurie, 1990, 30)

3. 'They are strong, dark, forbidding, almost primitive realizations of the psychological dramas within the tales', write J. Whalley and T. Chester (235).

V *Sendak and Disney*

1. 'I am setting a text to pictures, much as a composer sets a poem to music', writes Maurice Sendak (C, 8).
2. Interview on BBC television, 1982.
3. P. Nodelman, 1988, 273. Disney's animals are so closely aligned with types of All-American children they are hardly animals at all. Their physical characteristics speak loudly of 'conventional American gender attributes of the thirties and forties' (ib., 115).
4. *Snow White* was immensely successful: it broke all box office records during 1937-9; it was the first film to play at Radio City Music Hall for more than 3 weeks (its 5-week box office total was $525,000).

VI *Where the Wild Things Are*

1. Annie Pissard reckons (in "Long Live Barbar!") that few

illustrators can bring children alive in pictures. She notes that Maurice Sendak's Max borrows some of his liveliness from his wolf costume (1983-84, 71).

2. P. Nodelman, 1988, 178.
3. Readers tend to empathize with figures on the left in a picture: Maurice Sendak uses this in *Where the Wild Things Are*, having Max stand on the left when he's in his room conjuring up the magical forest. When he's making mischief, he is seen on the right; in *Outside Over There* Ida is seen on the left when the goblins are coming to steal her sister, but when she realizes the situation, she moves to the right. A character seen on the right creates a tension, between where they are and where they should be. So Max is seen to the right of the first Wild Thing he meets.
4. W. Moebius, 1986, in P. Hunt, 1990, 141.
5. At the beginning of the book, Max is shaded with hatching, while the objects around him are shaded with crosshatching. In the picture of Max's camp, the crosshatching speaks of nervous energy, as it covers much of the bedspread, the wallpaper and the knotted handkerchiefs. Max consists of more crosshatching as the forest grows in his room; during the wild rumpus, the shading is all crosshatching, except on Max, but he too becomes shaded with crosshatching as the sequence progresses. Significant, also, is the background, which is full of crosshatching in some of the early pictures, but a clear, pastel sky accompanies the wild rumpus pictures.
6. Paul Arakelian writes in the *Children's Literature Association Quarterly* that

   the text and drawings of *Wild Things* contribute to a subtle crescendo of mastery as the boy controls the wild things, and then a descrescendo as he returns to his room. As the size of the drawings increases and then shrinks, all sorts of other developments, as the metaphors of time and place, the topics of the illustrations, the compounding style of both text and drawing, also expand and contract, drawing us into this ordered, controlled experience. The entire enterprise – text, drawings, printing, story – becomes one metaphor for Max's going and coming. (126)

7. B. Bettelheim, in *Ladies Home Journal*, in AMS, 104.
8. W. Moebius, 1986, in P. Hunt, 1990, 137.
9. J. Kristeva, *Powers of Horror,* 1982, 157.
10. J. Kristeva, *Tales of Love*, 1987, 26.
11. S. Hekman, *Gender and Knowledge: Elements of a*

Postmodern Feminism, Polity Press,1990, 149.

VII In the Night Kitchen

1. M. Sendak: "A Conversation with Virginia Haviland", C, 174.
2. 'Sendak has masterfully done' writes S. Jones in *The Fairy Tale: The Magic Mirror of Imagination,*

   what fairy tales traditionally do; he presents an exaggerated externalized image of the protagonist's inner conflict. In this case, the conflict is with his own, wild or mischievous self... *Where the Wild Things Are* teaches a valuable moral lesson about acknowledging and coming to terms with one's emotional and instinctive impulses. (1995, 106-7)

3. M. Sendak, letter, 1969, in AMS, 174.
4. R. Graves, *The White Goddess*, Faber, London, 1961, 27f, 85.

VIII Outside Over There

1. Peter Hunt writes in *An Introduction to Children's Literature* that Maurice Sendak's work 'is highly allusive, as in Outside *Over There* (although the quality of his written text is questionable), and highly aware of the spatial codes available to the picture-book artist – notably in *Where the Wild Things Are*' (1994, 159).
2. The works of Philipp Otto Runge (such as his dialect tales *The Juniper Tree* and *The Fisherman and His Wife*) were the inspiration and model for the Grimm brothers. (J. Zipes, 1989, 12). Sendak began the artwork on December 27, 1976.
3. Julia Kristeva has commented on the depiction of folds in clothes in relation to the art of the Italian Renaissance painter Giovanni Bellini, in her wonderful essay on Bellini, "Motherhood According to Giovanni Bellini" (1975). Every Renaissance painter had to learn how to paint folds in clothes, and Bellini spent a good deal of time and effort producing deep, shadowy folds, 'the luminous folds and secret depths of the sacred', as Kristeva calls them (1982, 260). These folds are themselves part of the overall eroticization of the Virgin, and of motherhood.
4. S. Roxburgh, 1983-84, 21.

IX Maurice Sendak's Other Books

1. S. Roxburgh, 1983-84; P. Nodelman, 1988, 154.
2. E. Taylor: *German Popular Tales*, 1823, in J. Grimm, 1869.

X Maurice Sendak and Other Illustrators

1. Edward Ardizzone: *Little Tim and the Brave Sea Captain*, Kestrel Books, 1982.
2. E. Ardizzone: *Ardizzone's English Fairy Tales*, Andre Deutsch, London, 1980.
3. See, for example, P. Bruston's *The Castle of Fear*, Walker Books, London, 1986.
4. J. Willis & S. Varley: *The Monster Bed*, Beaver Books, 1988.
5. S. Jones writes:

   The Cat in the Hat uses the fantastic plot, symbolism, and themes characteristic of fairy tales to perform much the same function as traditional fairy tales – to provide its audience members with a functionalized means of confronting their most basic concerns. (1995, 104)

6. N. Jones: "Who will be the inspiration for our children now?", *Sunday Times*, Nov 20, 1994, 3, 7.

Bibliography

This is a selected bibliography only. Comprehensive bibliographies can be found elsewhere.

BOOKS BY MAURICE SENDAK

Kenny's Window, Harper & Row, New York, 1956
I Want To Paint My Bathroom Blue
Circus Girl, by Jack Sendak, 1957
Very Far Away, Harper & Row, 1957
A Kiss For Little Bear, by Else Minarik, Harper, 1958
The Moon Jumpers, by J.M. Udry, Harper & Row, 1959
Seven Tales, by Hans Christian Andersen, Harper & Row, 1959
The Sign on Rosie's Door, Harper & Row, 1960
What Do You Say, Dear? by Sesyle Joslin, HarperCollins, 1961
The Nutshell Library, Harper & Row, 1962
Chicken Soup with Rice: A Book of Months, Scholastic, New York, NY, 1962
Where the Wild Things Are, Harper & Row, 1963
She Loves Me, She Loves Me Not, by Robert Keeshan, HarperCollins, 1963
How Little Lion Visited Times Square, by Amos Vogel, HarperCollins, 1963
The Bee-Man of Orn, by F. Stockton, Holt, Rinehart & Winston, 1964
Pleasant Fieldmouse, by Jan Wahl, HarperCollins, 1964
Lullabies and Night Songs, by Alec Wilder, HarperCollins, 1965
Hector Protector and As I Went Over the Water, Harper & Row, 1965
Zlateh the Goat and Other Stories, by I.B. Singer, Harper & Row, 1966
Poems From William Blake's Songs of Innocence, by William Blake, Bodley Head, London, 1967
The Golden Key, by George MacDonald, Farrar, Straus & Giroux, 1967
Higglety Pigglety Pop! or There Must Be More to Life, Harper & Row, 1967
In the Night Kitchen, Harper & Row, 1970

Fantasy Drawings, Rosenbach Foundation, 1971
The Magician: A Counting Book, Rosenbach Foundation, 1971
Pictures by Maurice Sendak, Harper & Row, 1971
The Juniper Tree and Other Tales From Grimm, tr. L. Segal & R. Jarrell, Bodley Head, 1973
King Grisly-Beard: A Tale From the Brothers Grimm, tr. E. Taylor, Bodley Head, 1973
Fly By Night, by Randall Jarrell, Farrar, Straus & Giroux, New York, 1976
Seven Little Monsters, Harper & Row, 1976
Some Swell Pup, or Are You Sure You Want a Dog?, Harper & Row, 1976
Bat-Poet, by Randall Jarrell, Collier, 1977
Outside Over There, Harper & Row, 1981
Dear Mili, Viking Kestrel, 1988
Nutcracker, by E.T.A. Hoffmann, Crown, 1984
The Love of Three Oranges, by Frank Corsaro, Bodley Head, London, 1984
In Grandpa's House, Harper & Row, 1985
The Cunning Little Vixen, by Rudolph Tesnohlidek, Farrar, Straus, Giroux, 1985
Really Rosie; A New Musical, by Carole King, French, New York, NY, 1985
The Big Green Book, by Robert Graves, Macmillan, New York, NY, 1985
What Do You Say, Dear? by Sesyle Joslin, Harper & Row, 1986
The Griffin and the Minor Canon, by Frank Stockton, Harper & Row, New York, NY, 1986
Caldecott & Co.: Notes on Books and Pictures, Reinhardt/ Viking, 1988
Somebody Else's Nut Tree and Other Tales From Children, by R. Krauss, Linnet, Hamden, CT, 1990
I Saw Esau, Candlewick, Cambridge, MA, 1992
We Are All in the Dumps with Jack and Guy, HarperCollins, 1993
The Wonderful Farm, by Marcel Aymme, HarperCollins, 1994
The Miami Giant, by Arthur Yorkins, HarperCollins, 1995
Pierre, or The Ambiguities, by H. Melville, HarperCollins, 1995
Frank & Joey Go to Work, by Arthur Yorkins, HarperFestival, New York, NY, 1996
The Animal Family, by Randall Jarrell, HarperCollins, 1996
The Eventful History of Three Blind Mice, ed. M. Sendak & J. Reed, Oxford University Press, 1997
What Can You Do with a Shoe?, by Beatrice Shenk De Regniers, M. K. McElderry, New York, NY, 1997
Bumble-Ardy, 2011
"Mother Goose's Garnishings", in V. Haviland, 1973 (see below), 188-195

"Picture Book Genesis: A Conversation with Maurice Sendak", in M. Esmonde, 1979, 29-40
with V. Haviland: "Questions to an Artist Who is Also an Author", in V. Haviland, 1980, 25-46

OTHERS

G. Adams, ed. *The Cambridge Guide to Children's Books in English*, Cambridge University Press, Cambridge, 2003
B. Alderson: *Looking at Picture Books*, National Book League, Oxford, 1973
P. Arakelian: "Text and Illustration: A Stylistic Analysis of Books by Sendak and Mayer", *Children's Literature Association Quarterly*, 10, 3, Autumn, 1985
A. Arne: *The Types of Folk-tale*, Helsinki, 1961
B. Bader: *American Picturebooks From Noah's Ark to the Beast Within*, Macmillan, New York, 1976
J. Barr: *Illustrated Children's Books*, British Library, 1986
M. Barrier. *Building a Better Mouse: Fifty Years of Animation*, Library of Congress, Washington, D.C., 1978
P. Barron & J. Burley, eds. *Jump Over the Moon: Selected Professional Readings*, Holt, Rinehart & Winston, New York, NY, 1984
R. Bator, ed. *Signposts to Criticism of Children's Literature,* American Library Association, Chicago, 1983
J. Baudrillard: *Selected Writings*, Polity Press, 1988
C. Bazalgette & D. Buckingham, eds. *In Front of the Children: Screen Entertainment and Young Audiences*, BFI, London, 1995
L. Bechtel: "The Art of Illustrating Books For the Younger Readers", in V. Haviland, 1973, 173-6
E. Bell *et al*, eds. *From Mouse to Mermaid: The Politics of Film, Gender and Culture*, Indiana University Press, Bloomington, IN, 1995
D.I. Berland. "Disney and Freud: Walt Meets Id", *Journal of Popular Culture*, Spring, 1982
B. Bettelheim: *The Uses of Enchantment: The Meaning and Importance of Fairy Tales*, Knopf, New York, 1976
—. & K Zelan: *On Learning to Read: The Child's Fascination with Meaning*, Vintage, New York, 1982
D. Bland: *A History of Book Illustration*, Faber, 1958
—. *The Illustration of Books*, Faber, 1962
D. Blythe. *The Good, the Bad and the Ugly: Moral Ambiguity in the Tales of the Brothers Grimm,* Pauper's Press, 1993
G. Bodmer: "Ruth Kraus and Maurice Sendak's Early Illustration", *Children's Literature Association Quarterly*, 11, 4, Winter, 1986/7

R.B. Bottigheimer, ed. *Fairy Tales and Society: Illusion, Allusion and Paradigm*, University of Pennsylvania Press, Philadelphia, 1986
—. *Grimms' Bad Girls and Bold Boys: The Moral and Social Vision of the Tales,* Yale University Press, New Haven, 1987
O. Bozejovsky & V. Rawennoff, ed. *Modern European Children's Book Illustrators*, Bohem's Artists, Zurich, 1982
K. Briggs: *An Encyclopedia of Fairies*, Pantheon, New York, 1976
S. Brownmiller: *Men, Women and Rape* Bantham, New York, 1976
L. Burns: "Red Riding Hood", *Children's Literature*, 1, 1972
E. Byrne & M. McQuillan. *Deconstructing Disney,* Pluto Press, London, 1999
A. Campbell. *From "Goggle-Eyes" to "Harry Potter",* LISE Publications, 2000
J. Campbell: *The Hero With a Thousand Faces*, Paladin, 1978
H. Carpenter. *J.R.R. Tolkien: A Biography*, Allen & Unwin, London, 1977
—. *The Inklings: C.S. Lewis, J.R.R. Tolkien, Charles Williams, and Their Friends,* Allen & Unwin, London, 1978
—. & M. Prichard. *The Oxford Companion to Children's Literature*, Oxford University Press, Oxford, 1984/ 1999
A. Carter: *The Virago Book of Fairy Tales*, Virago 1991
J. Cech: "Remembering Caldecott", *Lion and the Unicorn*, 7/8, 1984
—. *Angels and Wild Things*, Penn State University Press, 1995
A.B. Chinen. *In the Ever After: Fairy Tales Second Half of Life,* Chiron Publication, Wilmette, IL, 1989
—. *Once Upon a Midlife: Classical Stories and Mythic Tales To Illuminate the Middle Years,* Jeremy P. Tarcher, Los Angeles, CA, 1992
A. Chamber: *Booktalk: Occasional Writing on Literature and Children*, Bodley Head, 1985
P. Cianciolo: *Illustration in Children's Books*, William Brown, Dubuque, Iowa, 1976
T. Coffin: *The Female Hero in Folklore and Legend*, Seabury, New York, 1975
A.M. Cohn: *George Cruikshank*, London, 1924
E. Cook: *The Ordinary and the Fabulous: An Introduction to Myths, Legends and Fairy Tales for Teachers and Storytellers*, Cambridge University Press, 1969
J.C. Cooper: *Fairy Tales: Allegories of the Inner Life*, Aquarian Press, 1983
J. Cott: *Pipers At the Gates of Dawn: The Wisdom of Children's Literature,* Random House, New York, 1983
—. *Beyond the Looking Glass: Extraordinary Works of Fairy Tale & Fantasy*, Stonehill, New York, 1973

H. Crago: "Who Does Snow White Look At?", *Signal*, 45, September, 1984

—. "The Roots of Response", *Children's Literature Association Quarterly*, 10, 3, Autumn, 1985

S. Culhane. *Talking Animals and Other People*, St Martin's Press, New York, NY, 1986

G. DeLuca: "Art, Illusion and Children's Picture Books", *Children's Literature Association Quarterly*, 9, 1, Spring, 1984

—. "Exploring the Levels of Childhood: The Allegorical Sensibility of Maurice Sendak", *Children's Literature*, 12, 1984

J. Doonan: "*Outside Over There*: A Journey in Style", *Signal*, 50, May, 1986

—. "Talking Pictures: A New Look at Hansel and Gretel", *Signal*, 42, September, 1983

Anne Duggan. *Salonnières, Furies, and Fairies,* University of Delaware Press, Newark, 2005

A. Dundes, ed. *Cinderella: A Casebook*, Garland, New York, 1982

—. "The Psychoanalytic Study of Folklore", *Annals of Scholarship*, 3, 1985

S. Egoff: *Thursday's Child: Trends and Patterns in Contemporary Children's Literature*, American Library Association, Chicago, 1980

—. & G.T. Stubbs *et al*: *Only Connect: Readings on Children's Literature*, Oxford University Press, New York, 1980

M. Eisner. *Work in Progress*, Penguin, London, 1999

M. Eliot. *Walt Disney: Hollywood's Dark Prince: A Biography*, Andre Deutsch, London, 1994

J. Ellis. *One Fairy Story Too Many: The Brothers Grimm and Their Tales*, University of Chicago Press, Chicago, IL, 1983

R. Ellwood. *The Politics of Myth: A Study of C.G. Jung, Mircea Eliade and Joseph Campbell,* State University of New York Press, Albany, NY, 1999

R.K. Engen: *Randolph Caldecott: "Lord of the Nursery",* Oresko Books, 1976

M. P. Esmonde & P.A. Ord, eds. *Proceedings of the Fifth Annual Conference of the Children's Literature Association, Harvard University, 1979*, Villanova University, Villanova, 1981

W. Evans-Wentz: *The Fairy-faith in Celtic Countries*, Oxford University Press, 1911

C.R. Farrer, ed. *Women and Folklore*, University of Texas Press, Austin, 1975

W. Feaver: *When We Were Young: Two Centuries of Children's Book Illustration*, Thames & Hudson, 1977

M.-L. von Franz: *An Introduction to the Interpretation of Fairy Tales*, Spring Publications, New York, 1970

—. *Problems of the Feminine in Fairy Tales,* Spring Publications, New York, 1972
—. *Introduction to the Psychology of Fairy Tales*, Spring Publications, New York, 1978
—. *Individuation in Fairy Tales*, Zurich, 1977
—. *The Psychological Meaning of the Redemption Motif in Fairy Tales*, Inner City Books, Toronto, 1980
E. Fromm: *The Forgotten Language: An Introduction to the Understanding of Dreams, Fairy Tales and Myths*, Grove Press, New York, 1957
R. Giddings & E. Holland. *J.R.R. Tolkien: The Shores of Middle-earth*, Junction Books, London, 1981
S.M. Gilbert & S. Gubar: *The Mad Woman in the Attic: The Woman Writer and the Nineteenth-century Imagination*, Yale University Press, New Haven, 1979
N. Gilpatrick: "Power of Picture Books to Change Child's Self-Image", in M. White, 1976
J. Goldthwaite. *The Natural History of Make-Believe: A Guide to the Principal Works of Britain, Europe, and America,* Oxford University Press, Oxford, 1996
M. Griffel & A. Block. *Operas in English: A Dictionary,* Greenwood Press, 1999
J. & W. Grimm: *German Popular Stories*, ed. Edgar Taylor, Hotten, 1869
—. *The Complete Grimm's Fairy Tales*, tr. M. Hunt & J. Stern, Pantheon, New York, 1972
—. *The Complete Fairy Tales of the Brothers Grimm*, tr. Jack Zipes, Bantam, New York, 1987
W.R. Halliday: *Indo-European Folk Tales and Greek Legend*, Cambridge, 1933
C. Hanks & D.T. Hanks: "Perrault's "Little Red Riding Hood": Victim of Revision", *Children's Literature*, 7, 1978
R.P. Harrison: *Forests: The Shadow of Civilization*, University of Chicago Press, Chicago, IL, 1992
R. Haughton: *Tales From Eternity: The world of faerie and the spiritual search*, Unwin, 1973
V. Haviland, ed. *Children and Literature: Views and Reviews*, Scott, Foresman, Glenview, IL, 1973
—. *The Openhearted Audience: Ten Authors Talk About Writing for Children,* Library of Congress, Washington, 1980
B. Hearne & M. Kaye, eds. *Celebrating Children's Books: Essays on Children's Literature in Honor of Zena Sutherland*, Lothrop, Lee & Shepard, 1981
R. Hein. *Christian Mythmakers: Lewis, L'Engle, Tolkien, Macdonald, Chesterton and Others*, Cornerstone Press, Chicago, IL, 1998
J. Heuscher: *A Psychiatric Study of Fairy Tales*, Thomas, Springfield, IL, 1963

R. Holliss & B. Sibley. *Mickey Mouse: His Life and Times*, Harper & Row, New York, NY, 1986

—. *The Disney Studio Story*, Crown Books, New York, NY, 1988

P. Hunt: *An Introduction to Children's Literature*, Oxford University Press, 1994

—. ed. *Children's Literature: The Development of Criticism*, Routledge, 1990

—. "Childist Criticism: The Subculture of the Child, the Book and the Critic", *Signal*, 43, January, 1984

—. "Questions of Method and Methods of Questioning Childist Criticism in Action", *Signal*, 45, September, 1984

B. Hürlimann: *Three Centuries of Children's Books in Europe*, Oxford University Press, 1967

H. Ide, ed. *Projekt Deutchunterricht*, 1, Metzler, Stuttgart, 1971

—. ed. *Projekt Deutchunterricht*, 6, Metzler, Stuttgart, 1974

L. Irigaray: *The Irigaray Reader,* ed. M. Whitford, Blackwell, Oxford, 1991

J. Jacobs: *English Fairy Tales*, Dover, New York, 1967

—. *More English Fairy Tales*, Shocken, New York, 1968

I. Jan: *On Children's Literature*, Allen Lane, 1973

H. Jenkins, ed. *Children's Culture Reader,* New York University Press, New York, NY, 1998

S.S. Jones. *The New Comparative Method: Structural and Symbolic Analysis of the Allomotifs of 'Snow White'*, Academia Scientiarum Fennica, Helsinki, 1990

—. *The Fairy Tale: The Magic Mirror of Imagination*, Twayne, New York, NY, 1995

R.A. Jordan & S.J. Kalcik, eds. *Women's Folklore, Women's Culture*, University of Pennsylvania Press, Philadelphia, PA, 1985

G. Jungblutt: "Märchen der Brüer Grimm – femministich glesen", *Diskussion Deutsch*, 91, October, 1986

B. Kiefer: "The Child and the Picture Book: Creating Live Circuits", *Children's Literature Association Quarterly*, 11, 2, Summer, 1986

L. Kingman *et al,* eds. *Illustrators of Children's Books 1967-1976*, Horn Books, Boston, 1978

D.L. Kirkpatrick: *20th Century Children's Writers*, Macmillan, 1978

D. Klemin: *The Art of Art For Children's Books*, Clarkson N. Potter, New York, 1966

U.C. Knoepflmacher. *Ventures Into Childhood: Victorian Fairy Tales and Femininity*, University of Chicago Press, Chicago, IL, 1998

M. Kolbenschlag. *Kiss Sleeping Beauty Goodbye: Breaking the Spell of Feminine Myths and Models*, Doubleday, New York, NY, 1979

J. Kristeva. "Motherhood According to Giovanni Bellini", in

1982
—. *Desire in Language: A Semiotic Approach to Literature and Art*, ed. Leon Roudiez, tr. Thomas Gora *et al*, Blackwell, 1982
—. *Powers of Horror: An Essay on Abjection*, tr. Leon S. Roudiez, Columbia University Press, New York, 1982
—. *The Kristeva Reader*, ed. Toril Moi, Blackwell, 1986
—. *Tales of Love*, tr. Leon S. Roudiez, Columbia University Press, New York, 1987
T. Kushner. *The Art of Maurice Sendak*, Abrams, New York, NY, 2003
L.E. Lacy: *Art and Design in Children's Picture Books*, American Library Association, Chicago, 1986
S. Landes: "Picture Books as Literature", *Children's Literature Association Quarterly*, 10, 2, Summer, 1985
S.G. Lanes: *The Art of Maurice Sendak*, Abrams, New York, 1980
—. *Down the Rabbit Hole: Adventures and Misadventures in the Realm of Children's Literature*, Atheneum, New York, 1976
A. Lang: *Custom and Myth*, London, 1884
—. *Myth, Ritual and Religion*, Longmans, Green, 1887
M. Lieberman: "'Some Day My Prince Will Come': Female Acculturation Through the Fairy Tale", *College English*, 34, 1972
M. Lochhead. *Renaissance of Wonder: The Fantasy Worlds of C.S. Lewis, J.R.R. Tolkien, George Macdonald, E. Nesbit and Others*, Canongate, Edinburgh, 1973
—. *The Renaissance of Wonder In Children's Literature*, Canongate, Edinburgh, 1977
W. Lorraine: "An Interview with Maurice Sendak", in S. Egoff, 1981
A. Lurie: *Don't Tell the Grown-Ups: Subversive Children's Literature*, Bloomsbury, 1990
M. Lüthi: *Once Upon a Time: On the Nature of Fairy Tales*, Indiana University Press, Bloomington, 1976
—. *The Fairy Tale as Art Form and Portrait of Man*, tr. John Erickson, University of Indiana Press, Bloomington, 1985
—. *The European Folktale: Form and Nature*, tr. John D. Niles, Institute for the Study of Human Issues, Philadelphia, 1982
D. MacCann & O. Richard: *The Child's First Books: A Critical Study of Pictures and Texts*, H.W. Wilson, New York, 1973
B.E. Mahony *et al*: *Illustrators of Children's Books 1744-1945*, Horn Books, Boston, 1947
C. Manlove. *Modern Fantasy*, Cambridge University Press, Cambridge, 1975
—. *The Fantasy Literature of England*, Macmillan, London, 1999
—. *From Alice to Harry Potter: Children's Fantasy in England:* Cyber-editions Corporation, 2003

D. Martin: *The Telling Line: Essays on Fifteen Contemporary Book Illustrations*, Julia MacRae Books, 1989
R. McGills. "Criticism in the Woods: Faiy Tales as Poetry", in P. Nodelman, 1983
R. McLean: *Victorian Book Design and Colour Printing*, Faber, 1972
J. May, ed. *Children and Their Literature: A Reading Book*, Children's Literature Association Publications, West Lafayette, 1983
M. Meek *et al*, eds. *The Cool Web: The Pattern of Children's Reading*, Bodley Head, 1977
C. Meigs *et al*: *A Critical History of Children's Literature*, Macmillan, 1953
R. Michaelis-Jena: *The Brothers Grimm*, Routledge, 1970
W. Mieder: *Tradition and Innovation in Folk Literature*, University Press of New England, 1987
—. ed. *Grimms Märchen-modern*, Reclam, Stuttgart, 1979
N. Mikkelsen: "Sendak, Snow-White and the Child as Literary Critic", papor, MLA 100, Washington DC, 1984
W. Moebius: "Introduction to Picturebook Codes", *Word & Image*, 2, 2, April, 1986
R. Moore: "From Rags to Witches: Stereotypes, Distortions and Anti-humanism in Fairy Tales", *Interracial Books for Children*, 6, 1975
E. Moss: *Part of the Pattern*, Bodley Head, 1986
—. *Picture Books for Young People, 9-13*, Thimble Press, 1985
L. Mourey: *Introduction aux contes de Grimm et de Perrault*, Minard, Paris, 1978
C. Moustakis: "A Plea for Heads: Illustrating Violence in Fairy Tales", *Children's Literature Association Quarterly*, 7, 2, Summer, 1982
P. Neumeyer, ed. *Image and Maker*, Green Tiger, La Jolla, 1984
P. Nodelman & J.P. Ya, eds. *Festschrift: A Ten Year Retrospective*, Children's Literature Association Publications, West Lafayette, 1983
—. "How Picture Books Work", *Image and Maker*, Green Tiger Press, La Jolla, 1984
—. "Expectations: Titles, Stories, Pictures", *Children's Literature Association Quarterly*, 9, 1, 1984
—. *Touchstones: Reflections on the Best of Children's Literature*, Purdue University Press, Lafayette, 3 vols, 1985-88
—. *Words About Pictures: The Narrative Art of Children's Picture Books*, University of Georgia Press, Athens, GA, 1988
I. & P. Opie: *The Classic Fairy Tales*, Paladin, 1980
—. *The Lore and Language of School Children*, Oxford University Press, 1959
P.A. Ord, ed. *Proceedings of the Eighth Annual Conference of*

the Children's Literature Association, University of Minnesota 1981, Iona College, New Rochelle, New York, 1982
L. Paul: "Enigma Variation: What Feminist Theory Knows About Children's Literature", *Signal*, 54, Sept, 1987
M.B. Peppard: *Paths Through the Forest: A Biography of the Brothers Grimm*, Holt, Rinehart and Winston, New York, 1971
P.M. Pickard: *I Could a Tale Unfold: Violence, Horror and Sensationalism in Stories for Children*, Tavistock, 1961
A. Pissard: "Long Live Barbar!", *The Lion and the Unicorn*, 77-8, 1983-84
Vladimir Propp: *Morphology of the Folktale*, tr. Laurence Scott, University of Texas Press, Austin, 1968
E.S. Rabkin: *The Fantastic in Literature*, Princeton University Press, 1976
M.D. Reed: "The Female Oedipal Complex in Maurice Sendak's *Outside Over There*", *Children's Literature Association Quarterly*, 11, 4, 1986-7
F. Ricklin: *Wishfulfilment and Symbolism in Fairy Tales*, Johnson Reprint Company, New York, 1970
A. Roiphe. *For Rabbit*, Free Press, New York, 2002
J. Rose: *The Case of Peter Pan, or the Impossibility of Children's Fiction,* Macmillan, 1984
G. Rouger, ed. *Contes de Perrault*, Garnier, Paris, 1967
S. Roxburgh: "A Picture Equals How Many Words? Narrative Theory and Picture Books for Children", *Lion and the Unicorn*, 7/8, 1983-84
J. Ryder: *Artists of a Certain Line: a selection of illustrators for children's books*, Bodley Head, 1960
R. Sale: *Fairy Tales and After: From Snow White to E.B. White*, Harvard University Press, Cambridge, Mass., 1978
R. Selden & S. Smedman: "The Art of the Contemporary Picture Book", in P. Ord, 1982
Z. Shavit: *The Poetics of Children's Literature*, University of Georgia Press, Athens, GA, 1986
T. Shippey. *The Road to Middle-earth*, Allen & Unwin, 1982
—. ed. *Essays and Studies 1990: Fictional Space: Essays On Contemporary Science Fiction*, Oxford University Press, Oxford, 1991
—. *J.R.R. Tolkien: Author of the Century*, HarperCollins, London, 2000
J.S. Smith: *A Critical Approach to Children's Literature*, McGraw-Hill, New York, 1967
E. Smoodin, ed. *Disney Discourse: Producing the Magic Kingdom*, Routledge, 1994
M. Soriano: *Les Contes de Perrault: Culture savante et traditions populaires*, Gallimard, Paris, 1968
—. "From Tales of Warning to Formulettes: The Oral Tradition

in French Children's Literature", *Yale French Studies*, 43, 1969
J.D. Stahl, ed. *The Lion and the Unicorn*, 19, 1, June, 1995
C. Steedman, ed. *Language, Gender and Childhood*, Routledge, 1985
—. *The Tidy House: Little Girls Writing*, Virago, 1982
M. Steig: "Reading *Outside Over There*", *Children's Literature*, 13, 1985
Z. Sutherland & B. Hearne: "In Search of the Perfect Picture Book Definition", in P. Barron, 1984
—. & M.H. Arbuthnot: *Children and Books*, Scott, Foresman, Glenview, IL 1977
Martin Sutton. *The Sin-Complex: A Critical Study of English Versions of the Grimms' Kinder- und Hausmärchen in the Nineteenth Century*, Brüder Grimm-Gesellschaft, Kassell, 1996
M. Tatar. *The Hard Facts of the Grimms' Fairy Tales*, Princeton University Press, Princeton, NJ, 1987
—. *Off With Their Heads: Fairy Tales and the Culture of Childhood*, Princeton University Press, Princeton, NJ, 1992
M. Agnes Taylor: "In Defence of the Wild Things", *Horn Book*, 46, 1970
J. Thomas: *Inside the Wolf's Belly: Aspects of the Fairy Tale*, Sheffield Academic Press, 1989
J.R.R. Tolkien. *The Monster and the Critics and Other Essays*, ed. C. Tolkien, Allen & Unwin, London, 1983
T. Todorov: *The Fantastic: A Structalist Approach to a Literary Genre*, tr. R. Howard, Cornell University Press, New York, 1975
M. Usrey: "Mother Goose Without Tears: Fantasy and Realism in Mother Goose Illustrations since 1865", in P. Ord, 1982
A. Ussher & C.I von Metzradt: *Enter These Enchanted Woods, An Interpretation of Grimm's Fairy Tales*, Dolmen, Dublin, 1957
R. Viguers & M. Dalphin. *Illustrators of Children's Books, 1946-1956,* Horn Book, 1958
J. Waller: "Maurice Sendak and the Blakean Vision of Childhood", *Children's Literature*, 6, 1977
J.L. Ward & M. Fox: "A Look at Some Outstanding Books for Children", *Children's Literature Association Quarterly*, 9, 1, Spring, 1984
M. Warner. *From the Beast to the Blonde: On Fairy Tales and Their Tellers*, Vintage, London, 1995
—. *No Go the Bogeyman: Scaring, Lulling and Making Mock*, Chatto & Windus, London, 1998
V. Watson, ed. *The Cambridge Guide To Children's Books in English*, Cambridge University Press, Cambridge, 2001
P. Whalen-Levitt: "Making Picture Books Real: Reflections on a

Child's-Eye View", *Children's Literature Association Quarterly*, 6, 4, 1981
J. Whalley & T.R. Chester: *A History of Children's Book Illumination*, John Murray, 1988
G. White: *Edward Ardizzone: artist and illustrator*, Bodley Head, 1979
M. White, ed. *Children's Literature: Criticism and Response*, Charles E. Merrill, Columbus, Ohio, 1976
I. Wojcik-Andrews, ed. *The Lion and the Unicorn, Children's Films* issue, 20, 1, June, 1997
J. Zipes. *Breaking the Spell: Radical Theories of Folk and Fairy Tales*, Heinemann, London, 1978
—. "Who's Afraid of the Brothers Grimm? Socialization and Politicization through Fairy Tales", *Lion and the Unicorn*, 3, Winter, 1979-80
—. *Fairy Tales and the Art of Subversion: The Classical Genre for Children and the Process of Civilization*, Heinemann, London, 1983
—. *Trials and Tribulations of Little Red Riding Hood: Versions of the Tale in Socio-Cultural Context*, Heinemann, London, 1983
—. *Don't Bet on the Prince: Contemporary Feminist Fairy Tales in North America and England,* Methuen, New York, NY, 1986
—. "The Enchanted Forest of the Brothers Grimm: New Modes of Approaching the Grimms' Fairy Tales", *Germanic Review*, 62, 1987
—. *The Brothers Grimm: From Enchanted Forests to the Modern World*, Routledge, New York, NY, 1989
—. "Towards a Theory of the Fairy-tale Film: The Case of *Pinocchio*", in I. Wojcik-Andrews, 1997
—. ed. *The Oxford Companion To Fairy Tales*, Oxford University Press, 2000
—. *Sticks and Stones: The Troublesome Success of Children's Literature From Slovenly Peter to Harry Potter*, Routledge, London, 2002
—. *The Enchanted Screen: The Unknown History of Fairy-tale Films*, Routledge, New York, NY, 2011
—. *The Irresistible Fairy Tale*, Prince University Press, Princeton, NJ, 2012

WEBSITES

Publishers' websites have some useful information: HarperCollins, Scholastic and Simon & Schuster. A lso: Rosenbach Museum & Library: rosenbach.org.

ARTS, PAINTING, SCULPTURE

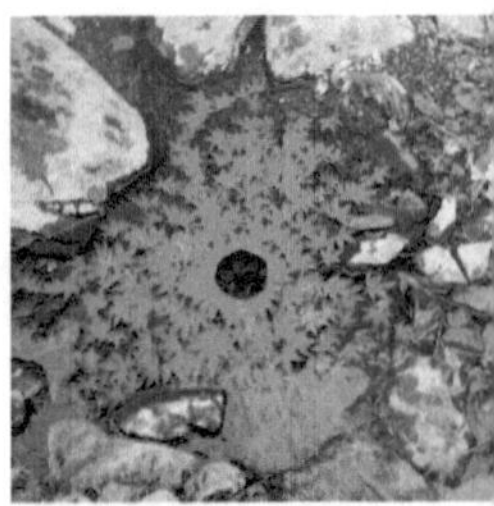

The Art of Andy Goldsworthy
Andy Goldsworthy: Touching Nature
Andy Goldsworthy in Close-Up
Andy Goldsworthy: Pocket Guide
Andy Goldsworthy In America
Land Art: A Complete Guide
The Art of Richard Long
Richard Long: Pocket Guide
Land Art In Great Britain
Land Art in Close-Up
Land Art In the U.S.A.
Land Art: Pocket Guide
Installation Art in Close-Up
Minimal Art and Artists In the 1960s and After
Colourfield Painting
Land Art DVD, TV documentary
Andy Goldsworthy DVD, TV documentary
The Erotic Object: Sexuality in Sculpture From Prehistory to the Present Day
Sex in Art: Pornography and Pleasure in Painting and Sculpture
Postwar Art
Sacred Gardens: The Garden in Myth, Religion and Art
Glorification: Religious Abstraction in Renaissance and 20th Century Art
Early Netherlandish Painting
Jasper Johns
Brice MardenLeonardo da Vinci
Piero della Francesca
Giovanni Bellini
Fra Angelico: Art and Religion in the Renaissance
Mark Rothko: The Art of Transcendence
Frank Stella: American Abstract Artist
Alison Wilding: The Embrace of Sculpture
Vincent van Gogh: Visionary Landscapes
Eric Gill: Nuptials of God
Constantin Brancusi: Sculpting the Essence of Things
Max Beckmann
Gustave Moreau
Caravaggio
Egon Schiele: Sex and Death In Purple Stockings
Delizioso Fotografico Fervore: Works In Process 1
Sacro Cuore: Works In Process 2
The Light Eternal: J.M.W. Turner
The Madonna Glorified: Karen Arthurs

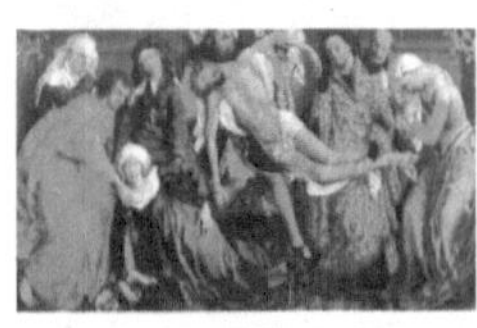

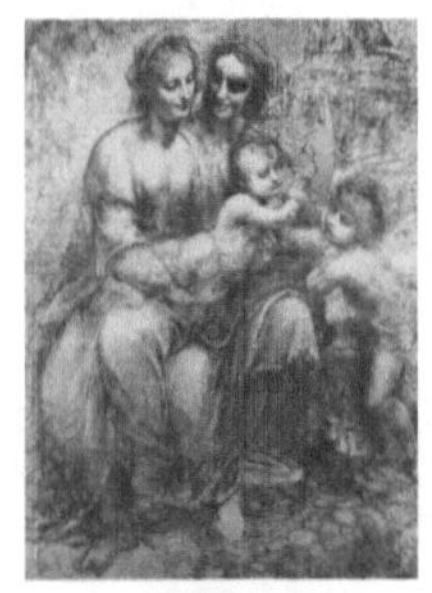

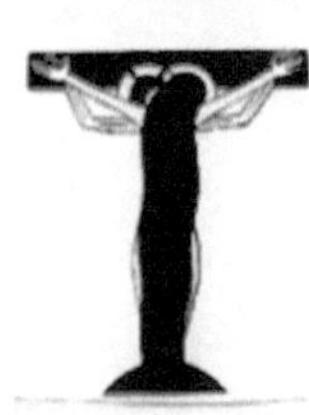

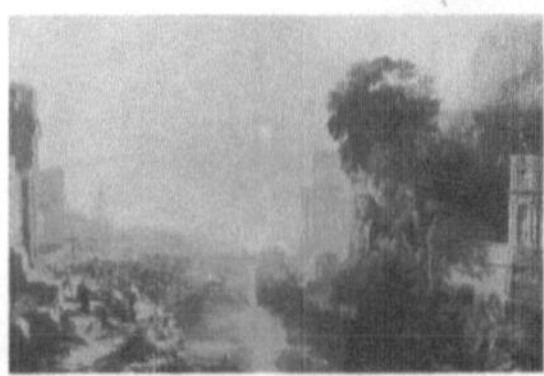

LITERATURE

J.R.R. Tolkien: The Books, The Films, The Whole Cultural Phenomenon
J.R.R. Tolkien: Pocket Guide
Beauties, Beasts and Enchantment: Classic French Fairy Tales
Tolkien's Heroic Quest
Brothers Grimm: German Popular Stories
Sexing Hardy: Thomas Hardy and Feminism
Thomas Hardy's *Tess of the d'Urbervilles*
Thomas Hardy's *Jude the Obscure*
Thomas Hardy: The Tragic Novels
Love and Tragedy: Thomas Hardy
The Poetry of Landscape in Hardy
Wessex Revisited: Thomas Hardy and John Cowper Powys
Wolfgang Iser: Essays and Interviews
Petrarch, Dante and the Troubadours
Maurice Sendak and the Art of Children's Book Illustration
Andrea Dworkin
Cixous, Irigaray, Kristeva: The *Jouissance* of French Feminism
Julia Kristeva: Art, Love, Melancholy, Philosophy, Semiotics and Psychoanalysis
Hélene Cixous I Love You: The *Jouissance* of Writing
Luce Irigaray: Lips, Kissing, and the Politics of Sexual Difference
Peter Redgrove: Here Comes the Flood
Peter Redgrove: Sex-Magic-Poetry-Cornwall
Lawrence Durrell: Between Love and Death, East and West
Love, Culture & Poetry: Lawrence Durrell
Cavafy: Anatomy of a Soul
German Romantic Poetry: Goethe, Novalis, Heine, Hölderlin
Novalis: *Hymns To the Night*
Feminism and Shakespeare
Shakespeare: *The Sonnets*
Shakespeare: Love, Poetry & Magic
The Passion of D.H. Lawrence
D.H. Lawrence: Symbolic Landscapes
D.H. Lawrence: Infinite Sensual Violence
The Ecstasies of John Cowper Powys
Sensualism and Mythology: The Wessex Novels of John Cowper Powys
Amorous Life: John Cowper Powys (H.W. Fawkner)
Postmodern Powys: New Essays on John Cowper Powys (Joe Boulter)
Rethinking Powys: Critical Essays on John Cowper Powys
Paul Bowles & Bernardo Bertolucci
Rainer Maria Rilke
Joseph Conrad: *Heart of Darkness*
In the Dim Void: Samuel Beckett
Samuel Beckett Goes into the Silence
André Gide: Fiction and Fervour
Jackie Collins and the Blockbuster Novel
Blinded By Her Light: The Love-Poetry of Robert Graves

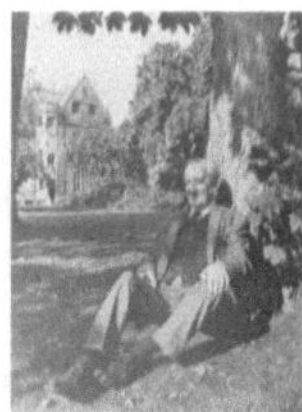
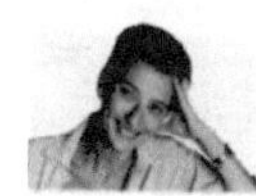
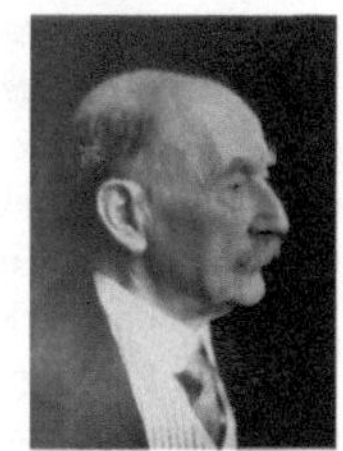
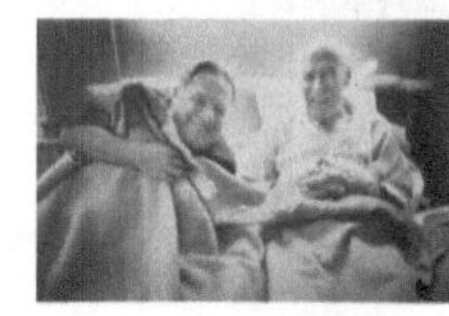
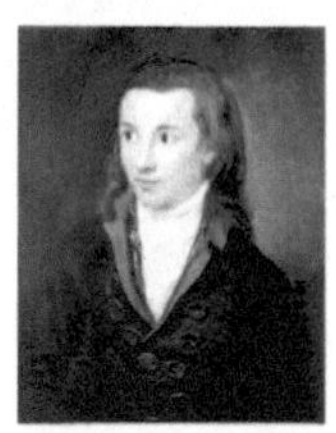

POETRY

Ursula Le Guin: *Walking In Cornwall*
Peter Redgrove: Here Comes The Flood
Peter Redgrove: Sex-Magic-Poetry-Cornwall

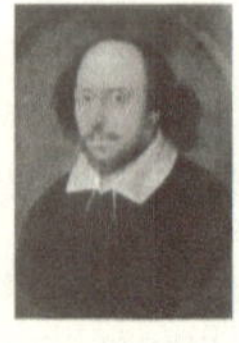

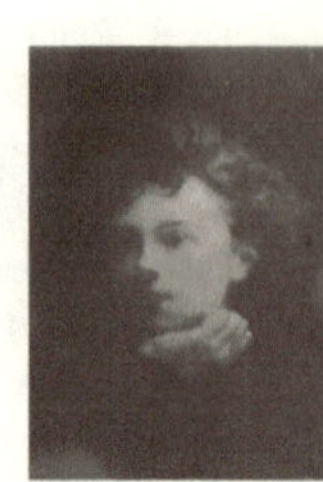

Dante: Selections From the *Vita Nuova*
Petrarch, Dante and the Troubadours
William Shakespeare: *The Sonnets*
William Shakespeare: Complete Poems
Blinded By Her Light: The Love-Poetry of Robert Graves
Emily Dickinson: Selected Poems
Emily Brontë: Poems
Thomas Hardy: Selected Poems
Percy Bysshe Shelley: Poems
John Keats: Selected Poems
John Keats: Poems of 1820

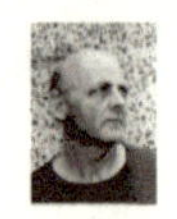

D.H. Lawrence: Selected Poems
Edmund Spenser: Poems
Edmund Spenser: *Amoretti*
John Donne: Poems
Henry Vaughan: Poems
Sir Thomas Wyatt: Poems
Robert Herrick: Selected Poems

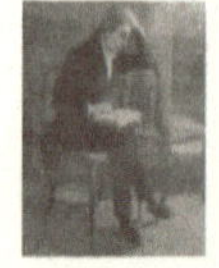

Rilke: Space, Essence and Angels in the Poetry of Rainer Maria Rilke
Rainer Maria Rilke: Selected Poems
Friedrich Hölderlin: Selected Poems
Arseny Tarkovsky: Selected Poems
Paul Verlaine: Selected Poems
Novalis: *Hymns To the Night*
Arthur Rimbaud: Selected Poems
Arthur Rimbaud: *A Season in Hell*

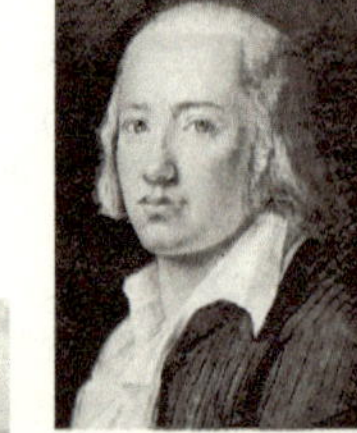

Arthur Rimbaud and the Magic of Poetry
D.J. Enright: By-Blows
Jeremy Reed: *Brigitte's Blue Heart*
Jeremy Reed: *Claudia Schiffer's Red Shoes*
Gorgeous Little Orpheus
Radiance: New Poems
Crescent Moon Book of Nature Poetry
Crescent Moon Book of Love Poetry
Crescent Moon Book of Mystical Poetry

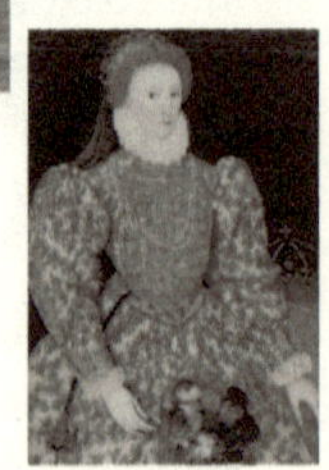

Crescent Moon Book of Elizabethan Love Poetry
Crescent Moon Book of Metaphysical Poetry
Crescent Moon Book of Romantic Poetry
Pagan America: New American Poetry

MEDIA, CINEMA, FEMINISM and CULTURAL STUDIES

J.R.R. Tolkien: The Books, The Films, The Whole Cultural Phenomenon
J.R.R. Tolkien: Pocket Guide
The *Lord of the Rings* Movies: Pocket Guide
The Ghost Dance: The Origins of Religion
The Cinema of Hayao Miyazaki
Hayao Miyazaki: *Princess Mononoke*: Pocket Movie Guide
Hayao Miyazaki: *Spirited Away*: Pocket Movie Guide
The Peyote Cult
Cixous, Irigaray, Kristeva: The *Jouissance* of French Feminism
Julia Kristeva: Art, Love, Melancholy, Philosophy, Semiotics and Psychoanalysis
Luce Irigaray: Lips, Kissing, and the Politics of Sexual Difference
Hélene Cixous I Love You: The *Jouissance* of Writing
Andrea Dworkin
'Cosmo Woman': The World of Women's Magazines
Women in Pop Music

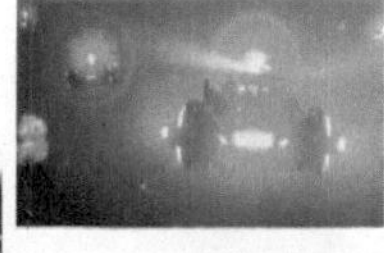

Discovering the Goddess (Geoffrey Ashe)
The Poetry of Cinema
The Sacred Cinema of Andrei Tarkovsky
Andrei Tarkovsky: Pocket Guide
Andrei Tarkovsky: *Mirror*: Pocket Movie Guide
Walerian Borowczyk: Cinema of Erotic Dreams

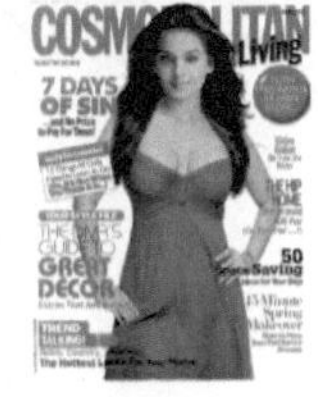

Jean-Luc Godard: The Passion of Cinema
Jean-Luc Godard: Pocket Guide
John Hughes and Eighties Cinema
Ferris Buller's Day Off: Pocket Movie Guide
The Cinema of Richard Linklater
Liv Tyler: Star In Ascendance

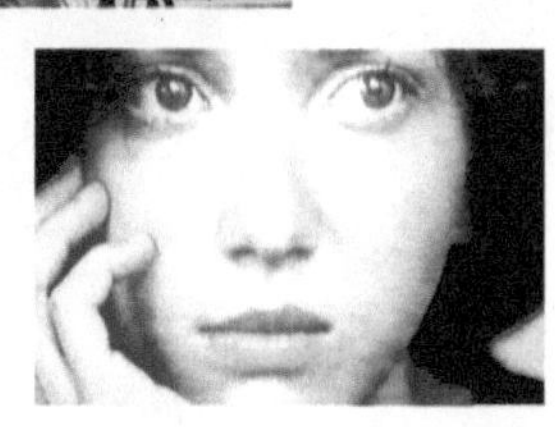

Blade Runner and the Films of Philip K. Dick
Paul Bowles and Bernardo Bertolucci
Media Hell: Radio, TV and the Press
Detonation Britain: Nuclear War in the UK
Feminism and Shakespeare
Wild Zones: Pornography, Art and Feminism
Sex in Art: Pornography and Pleasure in Painting and Sculpture
Sexing Hardy: Thomas Hardy and Feminism

The Light Eternal is a model monograph, an exemplary job. The subject matter of the book is beautifully organised and dead on beam. (Lawrence Durrell)

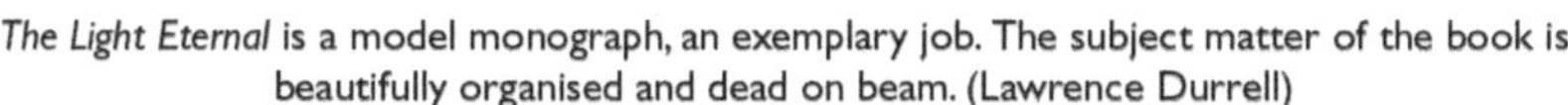

It is amazing for me to see my work treated with such passion and respect. (Andrea Dworkin)

Sex-Magic-Poetry-Cornwall is a very rich essay... It is like a brightly-lighted box. (Peter Redgrove)

CRESCENT MOON PUBLISHING P.O. Box 1312, Maidstone, Kent, ME14 5XU, England
0044-1622-729593 cresmopub@yahoo.co.uk www.crmoon.com

www.ingramcontent.com/pod-product-compliance
Lightning Source LLC
LaVergne TN
LVHW091148080826
845145LV00008B/2303

* 9 7 8 1 8 6 1 7 1 3 0 8 7 *